Resocialization:
An American Experiment

Resocialization Series

Sheldon R. Roen, Ph.D., Editor

Critical Incidents in Child Care
by Jerome Beker

Reference Group Theory and Delinquency
by Robert E. Clark, Ph.D.

Resocialization: An American Experiment
edited by Daniel B. Kennedy, Ph.D., and August Kerber, Ph.D.

Behavioral Threat and Community Response
by William C. Rhodes, Ph.D.

Residential Treatment of Emotionally Disturbed Children
edited by George H. Weber, Ph.D., and Bernard J. Haberlein, M.A.

From Dependency to Dignity
by Louis A. Zurcher, Ph.D., and Alvin E. Green, M.S.W.

RESOCIALIZATION:
AN AMERICAN EXPERIMENT

by
Daniel B. Kennedy
Campbell-Ewald Company and University of Detroit

and

August Kerber
Wayne State University

Behavioral Publications　　　　　New York
1973

HN65
.K45

Library of Congress Catalog Card Number 72-10326
Standard Book Number 87705-033-3 clothbound; 87705-091-0 paperbound
Copyright ©1973 by Behavioral Publications

BEHAVIORAL PUBLICATIONS, 2852 Broadway—Morningside Heights,
New York, New York 10025

Printed in the United States of America

Library of Congress Cataloging in Publication Data

Kennedy, Daniel B
    Resocialization: an American experiment.

    Bibliography: p.
    1. Socially handicapped--Rehabilitation--United
States. 2. Socialization. I. Kerber, August,
joint author. II. Title. [DNLM: 1. Cultural
deprivation. 2. Rehabilitation, Vocational.
3. Socialization. HN 65 K35r 1972]
HN65.K45   301.15'7   72-10326
ISBN 0-87705-033-3
ISBN 0-87705-091-0 (pbk)

PREFACE

This book describes a part of our society in a way that is seldom attempted. It is a study of the anatomy of failure. We have many exposes about social problems and issues, many diatribes and special pleadings from people who have particular points of view they wish to advocate. The woods are full of revisionism, reinterpretations, and latter day beatings of dead horses. The field of sociology owes much of its early development to a realistic inventory of hobohemias, or the lowest depths of our population, in various facets and classifications.

The twentieth century brought new polarities and exacerbated the old ones. The disgruntled or unemployed man could no longer head for the woods to find a new home and depend upon the land for his existence. The sick and incapable did not conveniently die rather soon. The thief was no longer beaten and kicked. Large wandering hordes of hopeless looking men and women appeared. The therapy of turning the soil to settle the malaise of soul gave way to clever men who tested with words and pencil and paper markings.

We had moved into an urbanized, technological world.

Still, like all societies, we had our alternate plans and strategies. In our society, the main strategy was resocialization. Much of twentieth century mankind is disjoined from human and physical resources. To get them back to viability, to "doing their thing," the agencies of our society utilize the strategy of resocialization. This "cures" the socially and morally ill and employs the unemployed.

This book is one of description. The authors began with the socialization process and moved to a discussion of how the process of socialization often fails. We then decided to discuss the nature of resocialization as it applies to some of our most important social institutions. The possible causes and theories of treatment of the academic underachiever are examined. The nature and processes of criminal recidivism, as well as theories of rehabilitation, are also subjected to study. Neither do the problems of hard-core unemployment in contemporary industrialized society escape scrutiny. Counseling and psychotherapy, which seem to have become the panacea of urban living, are also dealt with. Finally, certain conclusions are drawn. These conclusions may disappoint some but give encouragement to others.

Where do we go from here? That is another book. The authors believe that the description of the anatomy of failure is a very positive, constructive and, most important of all, a necessary step toward the obvious goal of social amelioration and integration.

CONTENTS

Preface   v
Introduction   1

CHAPTER I: THE NATURE OF SOCIALIZATION

A. What is Socialization?   4
B. How is it Accomplished?
    1. Nonverbal Responses   5
    2. The Meaning of Language   6
    3. The Acquisition of Language   7
    4. Primary and Secondary Groups   11
    5. The Effect of Mass Media   13
    6. Self-Socialization   15
C. The Concept of "National Character"   18
D. A Review   20
Footnotes   21

CHAPTER II: WHEN SOCIALIZATION "FAILS"

A. Missing the Objective
    1. Shortcomings   24
    2. Alternate Considerations
       a. The Relative Nature of Socialization   24
       b. The Question of Enculturation   25
    3. The Methodological Question   25
    4. Visible "Failures"   26
    5. The Responsibility of Society   28
B. The Development of Institutional Norms
    1. In Education   29
    2. In Criminolegal Systems   31
    3. In Industry   33
C. Societal Dissonance
    1. Ideal vs. Real Behavior   35

2. Restoration of Equilibrium   36
Footnotes   37

CHAPTER III: THE NATURE OF
RESOCIALIZATION

A. Resocialization as a Process
   1. Resocialization Defined   39
   2. A Dynamic Model of Resocialization   40
   3. Forms of Resocialization
      a. Compensatory Education   41
      b. Criminal Rehabilitation   42
      c. Training for the "Hard-Core" Unemployed   43
B. Socialization versus Resocialization
   1. A Table of Differences   43
   2. Interpretations   45
C. Resocialization in Contemporary Society
   1. History and Scope of Resocialization   48
   2. Analysis of Current Programs   49
Footnotes   49

CHAPTER IV: RESOCIALIZATION IN EDUCATION:
COMPENSATORY EDUCATION

A. Nature and Extent of the Problem
   1. The Culturally Disadvantaged Underachiever   50
   2. History and Scope of Compensatory
      Education   52
B. Theories on the Etiology and Treatment of
   Learning Disability
   1. Physiological   54
   2. Sociological and Psychological   57
   3. Institutional   68
C. An Analysis of Compensatory Education   76
Footnotes   82

CHAPTER V: RESOCIALIZATION IN CRIMINOLEGAL
SYSTEMS: CRIMINAL REHABILITATION

A. Nature and Extent of the Problem

1. The Recidivist   85
2. History and Scope of Criminal Rehabilitation   87
B. Theories on the Etiology of Criminal Behavior
1. Legalistic   90
2. Physical-Constitutional-Hereditary   91
3. Psychological   94
4. Sociological   98
C. Process and Theories of Criminal Rehabilitation
1. Choice of Milieu   101
2. Diagnosis   102
3. Treatment   103
4. A Working Typology   106
D. An Analysis of Criminal Rehabilitation   109
Footnotes   114

CHAPTER VI: RESOCIALIZATION IN INDUSTRY:
TRAINING FOR THE HARD-CORE UNEMPLOYED

A. Nature and Extent of the Problem
1. The Hard-Core Unemployed   118
2. History and Scope of Training for the
   Hard-Core Unemployed   120
B. Theories on the Etiology and Treatment of the
    Hard-Core Unemployed
1. Objective Factors   122
2. Subjective Factors   126
C. An Analysis of Training for the Hard-Core
    Unemployed   133
Footnotes   141

CHAPTER VII: COMMENTS ON THE USE OF
COUNSELING AND PSYCHOTHERAPY
IN RESOCIALIZATION

A. The Nature and Extent of Counseling and
    Psychotherapy
1. Definitions of Counseling and Psychotherapy 143
2. The Scope of Counseling and Psychotherapy   146
B. Counseling and Psychotherapy in Resocialization
1. Compensatory Education   149

2. Criminal Rehabilitation   150
3. Training for the Hard-Core Unemployed   150
C. An Analysis of Counseling and Psychotherapy   151
Footnotes   159

CHAPTER VIII:
CONCLUSIONS AND IMPLICATIONS

A. Contradictions in the Literature   161
B. A Method of Interpretation   164
C. The Question of Resocialization   168
D. The Promise of the Future
    1. The Nature of Behavior Therapy   170
    2. Resocializing the Current Generation   173
    3. Socializing the Next Generation   176
Footnotes   177

BIBLIOGRAPHY   179

TABLES AND FIGURES

Table: Socialization vs. Resocialization   44

Figures:
1. Word-Stimulus Association   8
2. Operant Conditioning   9
3. A Dynamic Model of Resocialization   40

INTRODUCTION

During the past decade, American society has become increasingly concerned about the inability of some of its members to function according to behavioral standards traditionally labeled "middle class." When real role behavior becomes too disparate from ideal role behavior, the dominant social institutions put into practice various programs of behavior intervention. The first phase of all such programs is to designate those individuals who are "inadequate" to fulfill roles prescribed for them. Then, through concentrated efforts on the part of teachers, social workers, and technicians, these individuals are prodded into understanding, accepting, and/or performing according to a desired pattern. Each institution has a different name for its program of behavior intervention. In education, there is the concept of "compensatory education." In criminolegal systems the notion of "criminal rehabilitation" is popular. Industry chooses to label its programs as "training for the hard-core unemployed."

To date, there has been a rather fragmented conception of these programs. They have been seen as distinct and separate from one another, both in theory and in practice. Training a slow learner to perform at grade level seems far removed from instructing the hard-core unemployed in the necessities of punctuality. Attempting to change the values of a chronic burglar appears even more unrelated. Yet, closer analysis reveals that all those activities have much in common and, in fact, operate from a similar theoretical basis. During the socialization process, dominant American

1

society attempts to instill in the individual the desire and ability to read and write, obey the law, and work to support self and family. Nonetheless, many are unable or unwilling to do so. They are either illiterate, criminal, chronically unemployed or all three. The process of socialization has not molded them according to the plan of the dominant society. In this event, such individuals are often submitted to resocialization programs wherein the respective institutions attempt to teach that which was not learned (or learned "improperly") during the original process of socialization.

Thus, compensatory education, criminal rehabilitation, and training the hard-core unemployed are all forms of resocialization. Although the specifics and circumstances may differ, the general principle remains the same. Resocialization programs operate on the assumption that values, attitudes, and ability can be permanently altered as a result of outside intervention. That is, it is possible either to teach an individual something which he has been subjected to but was unable or unwilling to learn, never been subjected to and never learned or, as the case may be, teach him that what he has learned is inappropriate.

The importance of resocialization, both to the individual and to society, is evidenced by the vast amounts of money and time being expended. Literally billions of dollars and rigorous effort by hundreds of thousands of individuals are devoted to various resocialization programs. Teachers, social workers, probation officers, vocational technologists, social researchers, and a myriad of other professionals operate on the notion that those whom they consider to be "inadequately" socialized can be resocialized as a result of behavior intervention. The magnitude of such efforts calls for continuous research in the theory, practice, and efficacy of resocialization. In this book we shall investigate resocialization in three institutional areas: education, criminolegal systems, and industry. The theories, processes, and efficacy of compensatory education, criminal rehabilitation, and training for the hard-core unemployed will be investigated in a descriptive/analytic fashion. An attempt will be made to answer such nonhypothesized questions as: What is socialization? Who decides that socialization has "failed"? What is resocialization? On what theories of etiology and treatment does resocialization operate? Are we effectively resocializing? Is resocialization a true goal of our society?

Before a full understanding of resocialization can be reached, one must be familiar with the dynamics of the process of socialization itself. Chapter I describes that process. Chapter II is concerned with reactions of the dominant society to those it considers poorly socialized. The definition, nature, and processes of resocialization are considered in Chapter III. The remainder of the book is more directly concerned with specific forms of resocialization. Each form of resocialization is considered separately and analyzed in research fashion. Definitions, history, extent, and theories of resocialization in each institutional area are presented, followed by an analysis of its over-all efficacy. There is also a chapter on counseling and psychotherapy which, in effect, are forms of resocialization. The book culminates in a chapter on conclusions and implications.

I. THE NATURE OF SOCIALIZATION

A. WHAT IS SOCIALIZATION?

The concept of socialization has been subjected to extensive and deliberate analysis. Definitions of socialization vary from lengthy and abstract paragraphs to terse statements of human behavior. Kimball Young defines socialization as "An interactional relationship by means of which the individual learns the social and cultural requirements that make him a functioning member of his society."[1] Psychologically, these relations concern habits, traits, ideas, perceptions, and values. Sociologically, the individual learns to conform to behavioral expectancies expressed by mores, folkways, and the normative traditions of his society. Another author considers socialization to be "the whole process by which an individual, born with behavior potentialities of enormously wide range, is led to develop actual behavior which is confined within a much narrower range—the range of what is customary and acceptable for him according to the standards of his group."[2] This definition pictures the socialization process as a form of "whittling," wherein a desired image is carved from human raw material by the knife of social interaction.

Still another social scientist defines socialization as a process by which "an individual internalizes the norms of his groups so that a distinct 'self' emerges, unique to this individual."[3] Through this process he acquires attitudes, goals, patterns of response, and a deep-abiding concept of the sort of person he is. One writer defines socialization as simply "the process of becoming a member of society"[4] whereas another chooses to render the following

4

definition: "A sociopsychological process whereby the personality is created under the influence of the educational institutions; a process intertwined with (a) the institutions wherein the general conditioning process relates itself to the school process, the family, play groups, racial groups, community, church, motion pictures and the like—and with (b) some problems of the sociology of groups formed in the educational process, and of the groups engaged in education . . ."[5]

After having read these definitions, one wonders whether they are intended to describe the same phenomenon or whether each successive author had discovered a unique social principle which necessitated the formulation of a new definition. As Sorokin suggests, however, these variations in definition are more the result of idiosyncratic motives than differing epistemological notions.[6] Instead of adding another definition of socialization to this already voluminous list, the reader will be offered the chance to form his own opinions. In the following pages, the social experiences which form the human being will be described. Although a total analysis of the socialization process would require volumes, it is possible to touch upon its major aspects. Let us begin with the writings of George Herbert Mead.

B. HOW IS IT ACCOMPLISHED?

1. Nonverbal Responses

Mead was a member of the University of Chicago faculty for many years and devoted a great amount of time to the investigation of socialization. After careful study, Mead was able to postulate several tenets which he felt essential to any comprehension of the process. To begin with, he felt that language is a biologically given potential of man and that this potential could only be developed through social interaction.[7] Before the development of language, however, nonverbal communication must take place. Mead believed that such communication, based on gestures, must be well-established in the developing infant if he is to grasp the intricacies of symbolic interaction. Examples of these behavioral phenomena include fondling, play activity, corporal punishment, and physical manipulation. Although some of these events are not necessarily communicative from the adult point of view, they are capable of instilling such feelings as affection, security, or fear in the mind of a child. The importance of this nonverbal communication has not been underemphasized by subsequent writers in the field. Shibutani believes that the gestures of the mother that a child perceives can greatly determine his personality. If the child feels he is the object of a selfish love, he will develop a low self-esteem. If, on the other hand, the child feels he is loved for his individual worth, a high self-esteem will develop. Although such feelings are nurtured on the verbal level, they are often nonverbal in origin.[8]

Complexities of nonverbal communication in the animal world have been well explored. The famed ethologist, Konrad Lorenz, devotes a great deal of his book *On Aggression* to the meaning of signs and gestures of subhuman species.[9] On the human level, Edward Hall devoted an entire book to an analysis of nonverbal communication.[10] Needless to say, the validity of Mead's assumptions about the importance of nonverbal communication is well established.

2. The Meaning of Language

Nevertheless, Mead places greater emphasis on the importance of language. Language and its symbols make possible ideas and communication of ideas. Because the human mind is superior and more complex than that of other beings, it is able to replace behavior with ideas. Though the mother can teach her child the meaning of "I am angry" only by behaving in appropriate ways, once the child masters the words the mother need not behave in an angry fashion to communicate anger.[11] Because the child already has experienced the mother's words-behavior sequence, he knows how his mother feels. It is at this point that the mother and child share an idea. Furthermore, having the idea of anger, the child can sense it outside of the context in which it was learned. By storing a number of these ideas and learning to understand them at various times, the child is developing "mind." As he develops and defines the meaning of anger and applies it to his own behavior, he acquires a self.[12]

A crucial element in the preceding discussion is the transformation of actual behavior into ideas. Perhaps this process could be more easily understood if one were familiar with the psychological concepts of stimulus-response, instrumental learning, positive reinforcement, and punishment.

3. The Acquisition of Language

Psychologists believe there are two kinds of elementary learning; classical and instrumental. Classical learning was first explored by the Russian physiologist Pavlov in 1927. By making small openings in the cheeks of a dog, he was able to measure the amount of saliva produced when the subject observed food. By sounding a tuning fork immediately prior to producing the food, the dog eventually associated the sound with food. After a few trials, the dog began to salivate at the sound of the fork alone.[13] The food was termed an "unconditioned stimulus" because it had the ability to elicit a subject's response without prior training. Thus, when the meat was presented to the dog, a salivary reflex was produced. This is termed "unconditioned response." The tuning fork is called a "conditioned stimulus" because it did not initially elicit a response. It came to do so after being paired with the unconditioned stimulus. The salivary response produced by the tuning fork is called a "conditioned response" because it is a learned response dependent upon the previous pairing of stimuli.[14] In order to relate this type of elementary learning to the development of the human language, let us examine Figure 1.

In this figure, the human being is subjected to the unconditioned stimulus of pain while at the same time he registers the conditioned stimulus of the word-symbol

Figure 1. Word-Stimulus Association

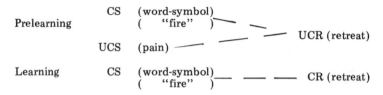

"fire." His response is unconditioned retreat during prelearning. On a second occasion, however, when he is presented with the conditioned stimulus, the word "fire," his conditioned response is also retreat. He has learned and can now respond to the symbol alone. Recalling our earlier discussion of the boy who sensed anger in his mother, we now see how he can respond to her conditioned stimuli (words) without having to again encounter the unconditioned stimulus of angry behavior. As the human mind develops, conditioned responses become more than just physical. Eventually, man's superb brain allows ideas, abstractions, and emotions to become conditioned stimuli capable of eliciting the most complex and varied responses.

The second type of elementary learning is referred to as "instrumental" and was first explored in this country by B. F. Skinner. In instrumental learning, the subject is more active than in classical learning. Whereas Pavlov's dog made a response to a stimulus, the subject in instrumental learning first makes a response and then receives a stimulus. Skinner conducted his experiments by placing a rat in a specially equipped box. By pure chance, a rat will eventually press a bar causing a pellet of food to fall into his dish. The food is a positive reinforcement to the act of pressing the bar. In this case, positive reinforcement is so defined because it strengthens the response which preceded it (bar-pressing). After consuming the pellet of food, the rat presses the bar at a greater rate.[15] Figure 2 diagrams the instrumental learning sequence.

The experimenter can also induce discrimination in his subject by presenting food only if the bar is pressed while a light is on. The response is reinforced if the light is on; not reinforced if the bar is pressed in the dark. Eventually,

Figure 2. Operant Conditioning[16]

Response   ---- Positive Reinforcement   ---- Increase in Strength
(Bar-pressing)   (food)   of Response

the rat will make his response (bar-pressing) only under certain conditions (light is on).[17] After thus familiarizing ourselves with instrumental learning, we can now relate the process to human behavior. Let us suppose the human child wanders into his parents' bedroom and is greeted with a show of affection. Because this can be interpreted as a positive reinforcement, he will do it again and again. Since human behavior becomes highly verbal with maturation, the child may use language as a response, perhaps saying "I love you" to the mother. If she positively reinforces this response, either symbolically or physically, the child will be prone to increase these responses. In this way, a child learns what behavior is acceptable in his immediate life-space.

On the other hand, a child's behavior may be punished. Punishment is any stimulus which tends to weaken the response preceding it. For example, a rat in the Skinner box might be given an electric shock when he presses the bar. This would eventually stop him from making such a response. We can relate this to human behavior by again considering the child. If, upon entering his parents' bedroom, he is greeted by symbols of anger, he will be disinclined to re-enter in the future.

Skinner was also able to produce response discrimination in his subjects. This phenomenon, explained earlier, is of prime importance to the developing human. The Skinner rat learned to push the bar only when the light was on. Human beings must also learn similar discriminatory behavior. For example, a child learns to say or do things only under certain conditions. He might say "Mrs. Jones is fat" when only his mother is present, but never when Mrs. Jones herself is present. He is taught this response discrimination by the application of reinforcement and punishment, be it on a physical or verbal-symbolic level. If he says "Mrs. Jones is fat" to his mother when she is alone, he may get positive reinforcement (laughter, hug) or none at all. In either case there is a chance he would repeat it. If Mrs. Jones is present, however, and he makes this response, he may be punished and, therefore, would be disinclined to repeat it in front of her. In any event, the child comes to learn those social conditions under which he may make certain responses.

Certainly, the preceding discussion of the etiology of language and ideas in the human has been greatly simplified. The evolution from a simple stimulus-response or response-reinforcement pattern to a mutually understood system of linguistic and behavioral symbols is highly complex. It is the ability of the human mind to grasp and retain these complex relationships which places mankind so far above the animal. The psychoneurological function of the human brain is to call upon literally millions of imprinted learning experiences, determine what the response or reinforcement was, and dictate appropriate action. Further explanation of the thinking process might better be left to the physiological psychologist, not to the sociologist.[18] For, at this level of abstraction, it is difficult to distinguish testable hypotheses from runaway theory.

The importance of language and its function in human society cannot be overestimated. Language is a collection of symbols having mutually understood meanings to its speakers. The symbols constituting language are the units in which a person thinks. Without these units (words) a person can only feel. He is not capable of planning, evaluating, or consciously and deliberately conveying meaning. Without words to facilitate and organize thought, a person can only live in the present. He cannot remember a past or conceptualize a future. The lack of symbols available to a child explains why most of our childhood memories are necessarily vague. With no linguistic symbols to hold and manipulate experience, few events are logically recorded.[19] Even in adults, the perception and recording of symbols must be organized to a considerable extent if there is to be any ready recall. It is because dreams occur during a period of psychic disorganization that few of them are completely remembered.

Thus it seems evident that language permits us to think.

Yet, it does even more. It provides categories and systems by which the human perceives reality. The noted linguist Edward Sapir made the following statements over forty years ago:

> "Language is a guide to social reality ... It is quite an illusion to imagine that one adjusts to reality essentially without the use of language and that language is merely an incidental means of solving specific problems of communication or reflection. The fact of the matter is that the 'real world' is to a large extent unconsciously built up on the language habits of a group. No two languages are ever sufficiently similar to be considered as representing the same reality. The worlds in which different societies live are distinct worlds, not merely the same world with different labels attached."[20]

4. Primary and Secondary Groups

Aware of the importance of language to thinking and personal development, we must examine the social situation in which it is fostered. According to Charles H. Cooley, the primary group is responsible for the initial inculcation of language and perceptions. Cooley defined primary groups as "those characterized by intimate face-to-face association and cooperation."[21] He went on to say that they are fundamental in forming the social nature and ideals of the individual. As a result of intimate association, individualities fuse into a common whole so that one's very self, for many purposes, is one with the group. Cooley describes this wholeness as a "we" and feels it is essential to the development of a healthy human personality. The most important primary groups are the family, playgroup, and neighborhood community group although there may be others.[22] In these groups, the maturing child is subjected to a unique set of patterns, personalities, and symbols. Although few primary groups in any one culture are so divergent as to be mutually unintelligible, there is a certain degree of idiosyncrasy. Just as every personality is different, every primary group is unique and will develop a personality according to its own collective pattern. A major principle responsible for this molding is what Cooley calls the "looking-glass self." In

Human Nature and the Social Order, Cooley explains that "a self-idea of this sort seems to have three principal elements: the imagination of our appearance to the other person; the imagination of his judgment of that appearance; and some sort of self-feeling, such as pride or mortification."[23] By conceptualizing what others think of him, the individual is able to assess his standing in a group. Recalling our earlier discussion about positive and negative reinforcements, we see how the "looking-glass self" develops personality. If the individual feels a sense of pride in his standing (positive reinforcement), he will continue to function as in the past. Should he be mortified (punished) he may either attempt to change his behavior or otherwise adjust the situation. It is important to note that this reflected self is not alien to the individual personality but is part of it. In fact, it generally plays the most important role in developing a person's attitude towards himself and others. We must not conclude from all of this that the social processes within the primary group are totally prescriptive or unilateral. The group is always differentiated and somewhat competitive. In Cooley's words, "The individual will be ambitious, but the chief object of his ambition will be some desired place in the thought of others and he will feel allegiance to common standards of service and fair play. So the boy will dispute with his fellows a place on the team, but above such disputes will place the common glory of his class and school."[24]

Mead expanded the "looking-glass self" and its function in human development with his concept of "generalized other." This "generalized other" is an individual's total impression of the judgments and expectations other people have of him. These "others" are not necessarily his primary group but might composes a cross section of the society in which he lives. He then looks at himself as though he were one of these persons and judges his actions and appearance according to those judgments of his "generalized other."[25] This theory may be illustrated through an analysis of children's play activities. At first, a child merely imitates the actions of his elders with little realization of why they act the way they do. Later in his development, in such games as hide-and-seek, he makes a partial response to the thinking of others by trying to guess where they thought to hide and by hiding himself where he thinks they might not look. Later, with the organized game, he learns that all participants have been assigned a particular role according to which they must act. As he reflects on how others are playing their role, he realizes that they too are observing his behavior in the light of role expectations. Even when nobody is near, the individual is never truly alone. Always in his mind he is responding to a pattern of behavior which he believes is expected of him. This explains much of man's otherwise nonpragmatic behavior. For example, why would a man leave an exorbitant tip in a restaurant he would never revisit? Why would he be embarrassed if he burped in a room full of strangers? Finally, why are so many of us cautious enough to employ proper grammar when we know we could convey our meaning just as effectively in the vernacular? The answer to these questions is in the mind of man. Every action we take is weighed against a behavior standard incorporated into our thinking. This standard may be called "conscience," "morality," or even "superego." Whatever the label, man's conception of right and wrong has been socially determined.

5. The Effect of Mass Media

In the "gesellshaft" society of contemporary America, there are important socializing variables which did not exist in the past. The most notable of these are the mass media. The developing human is subjected to a variety of ideas and opinions even before he learns to read. The television and radio industries in America present microcosms of human life which, although meant primarily to entertain, also serve a didactic purpose as well. Since the human, particularly the young human, develops a conception of life primarily as a result of the interactions he is a part of and observes, any symbol-emitting situation to which he is exposed could affect the structure of his world. Society is aware of this fact and has taken certain steps to control the socializing effects of mass media. All stations are under federal and state censorship and must subscribe to codes of ethics. This control seems to have come about largely as the result of public criticism of mass media. Social scientists have been no less harsh. Riesman sees a great deal of harmful social deviancy resulting from the shift to "other-direction" in American society. He believes that the American people are losing a pattern of controlled and purposeful social behavior and developing an incoherent, contradictory, and unstable system of values which leads an individual to rely on others more than himself.[26] Certainly, many critics have suggested that the "other-directed" man is a prime tool of, or even the result of, the many forms of mass media extant in society.

Merton proposes a different explanation for social deviancy. He contends that a culture must not extoll certain success-goals as universally desirable and then make access to these goals difficult or impossible for substantial segments of the population.[27] Should this happen, a profound sense of frustration will affect the society, spawning deviant and adjustive behavior often inimical to both the culture and the individual within it. Mass media have been accused of planting ideas and aspirations in the minds of those individuals whose position in society makes many things unattainable. A typical example is that of the impoverished youth who, with only limited experiences available to him, relies on the television set for excitement, entertainment, and even codes of ethics. Seeing the hero succeed and possess such culturally extolled things as wealth and property, the youth first identifies with him and then sets out to succeed himself. The real world, however, is different from the television studio and there are more failures than successes.[28]

Many writers have been content to criticize the effects of mass media on the developing child (and on the full-grown adult). However, social scientists, Kerber and Smith, find a great deal of educative merit attributable to mass media. The mass media produce what these writers call a "mass-culture." Although they make no attempt to whitewash any negative aspects of this culture, they do consider some of its useful functions. First, mass culture interprets the mores and and folkways of general culture.[29] The individual will often find himself in fragmented and strange groups as a result of the industrialized and urbanized society of today. To understand what is happening outside of one's frame of reference, and internalize transcultural values, mass media are necessary.

Mass media also induce standardization of values. The idealized values in our society are constantly discussed or implied by our mass media.[30] They are presented in a concentrated, thorough, often idealized form predigested to ensure intelligibility. Newspapers and broadcasting stations air many of the social conflicts and problems of the day. Particularly within the past decade, media have reminded the American public of their stated doctrine of equality and then chided them for falling short of declared goals.

Finally, Kerber and Smith argue that the mass media create unity and a common culture. American accomplishments, such as the moon landing, can be broadcast to the entire population. The man in the street has little opportunity to participate directly in such significant events, yet mass media allow him to become a direct observer. This makes for empathy and allows the unity that comes from mutual interest and involvement. Mass media also help to inform the public and can give them the background information necessary for concerted public action. The citizenry can better relate to one another because they have come to know one another. Mass media forge a common language, a common stock of gestures, social patterns, and a host of mutually intelligible symbols. The media provide a broad avenue for acculturation on a national level.[31]

6. Self-Socialization

Although social scientists attribute the greatest part of an individual's personal development to the social

situations into which he has been placed, it would be a
mistake to assume that the individual has no choice in the
matter of his own socialization. Great research and
theoretical emphasis is placed on the child in the
socialization process, little on the adult. Yet, socialization
is continuous through life and the individual must build on
his childhood experiences if he is to live in a rapidly
changing, heterogeneous society. Adults must change and
must socialize into newly developing roles.[32]

At a certain point in life, the maturing young human
begins to break away from the expectations or demands of
his primary groups. Although, in the final analysis, an
individual may still measure his actions by peer-group
values, he himself also becomes a judge of his own
behavior. Perhaps the first serious elements of self-
socialization begin in adolescence when the individual
breaks from his first primary group—the family. At this
point in life, the individual sees himself and his desires as
separate from his parents; not necessarily different, but
separate.[33] He realizes that he is an entity apart from
them and considers it important to the development of his
own ego that he be the independent determinant of his
behavior. Many adolescent psychologists believe this clash
with adult authority is necessary for personality development.[34] Still, however, the individual relies on a peer
group with which to test his ideas and behavior. The group
is fortified by an "in-group" feeling, a belief that they
must stand together if they are to throw off the "shackles"
of adult influence. Yet, even the influences of this peer
group tend to diminish as the individual approaches
adulthood. If he fails to become relatively independent of
them, he will be subject to ridicule by those older than he,
and often by any female who seeks his undivided
attention. Eventually, as he enters his early twenties, he
realizes that status is often inversely related to peer
dependence.

How then does an individual come to make certain
social choices in his life? What are the processes involved?
To answer these questions, one must first consider the
concept of "reference group" and "anticipatory

socialization." Krech, Crutchfield, and Ballachey define the reference group as "Any group with which an individual identifies himself such that he tends to use the group as a standard for self-evaluation and as a source of his personal values and goals. The reference groups of the individual may include both membership groups and groups to which he aspires to belong."[35] The individual chooses for himself a group, often loosely defined and composed, according to whose standards he wants to live. For example, he may admire the life-style of corporation executives and want it for himself. Although he does not necessarily know a "group" of executives, he imagines what such a group would expect. As a result of the interplay between the unique ego formed in the peer group and the peer group itself, a set of preferences is developed.[36] The peer group alone did not force this choice; the unique ego of every human being makes a major contribution. Through selective perception and selective exposure, an individual acts to reinforce any choice he may have made.

Having thus settled on a reference group, the individual engages in "anticipatory socialization." This can be defined as a process by which the individual prepares himself for acceptance into a group in terms of its required values, abilities, and roles. If the individual believes he does not satisfy entrance requirements, he works to gain those things which will qualify him. Once he has them, he works to ensure their continuous possession, particularly in a rapidly changing society. Thus, men conduct their affairs according to the requisites of a group (or groups) they have chosen for themselves. Some believe their reference group places great emphasis on religious purity and will so conduct themselves. Others feel they must display great money-making ability and will endeavor to become rich. A reference group may require nothing more than the assumption of a role. Newlyweds, commissioned officers, and Presbyterian ministers all learn the entry requirements of their reference groups and perform accordingly.

Certainly the process of socialization in adulthood is not as pat or smooth as it has been depicted here. Many individuals never choose a reference group or, if they do, lack the motivation to work at satisfying the entrance requirements. Still others may change reference groups so often as to preclude any possibility of a normal psychic life. Nevertheless, the individual himself plays an important role in the development of his social personality and should not be considered as purely and solely "a product of his environment."

C. The Concept of "National Character"

In many discussions of the socialization process, the question of "national character" is raised. Some anthropologists and many laymen believe the English are sportsmanlike and conventional, the Japanese intelligent and industrious, and the Italians artistic and impulsive. The rationale for such convictions appears to be that individuals socialized in a particular culture will develop personalities as unique as that culture. Margaret Mead, Ruth Benedict, Abraham Kardiner, and others have devoted a great deal of energy to the study of personality development in various cultures. Studies have asserted that certain Indian tribes are successful in instilling a lack of self-confidence and a suspicious nature in their children. Another tribe frowns on any form of competition by its members. Certainly, such findings may be valid when restricted to the research situation, but too often they are generalized to modern heterogeneous societies.

Smelser and Smelser define a nation as a subdivision of mankind living under sovereign government and within a circumscribed geographical area. In relation to this definition, it is noted that national and cultural boundaries do not correspond, thus increasing the complexity of any subsequent discussion.[37] For a definition of national character, we turn to Inkeles and Levinson: ". . . relatively enduring personal characteristics and patterns that are modal among adult members of a society."[38] It is understood that certain societies, through their institutions, call for certain behavior at certain times. For example, American enterprise must be viewed in light of our free enterprise, competitive economy; Russian irreligiosity must be interpreted in terms of a Communistic, atheistic government; and Spanish religiosity must be related to the monopolistic position of the church. One cannot assume the behavior of foreign nationals to be the direct result of narrow personality traits; he must look carefully at the societal ways of life and the demands of its institutions.[39]

According to Inkeles and Levinson, there have been three basic approaches to the study of what is supposed to be a national character: personality assessment of individuals, collective adult phenomena, and child-rearing systems.[40] Apparently, many results of these studies, often claiming the existence of a national character, have been accepted too readily and without careful analysis of the research methods used. Personality assessments are often made without benefit of adequate sampling or do not employ appropriate psychometric measures. Furthermore, the use of projective personality tests does not adequately compensate for cultural or ethnocentric qualities of the observer.[41]

Studies of collective adult phenomena such as plays and novels and examinations of folklore and myths do not necessarily represent the entire population. One must examine the cultural process involved in the production of plays, for example. A play is most often written by a unique individual, sold to a unique producer, and usually geared to affect a selected audience. The danger of generalizing from literary or visual phenomena is obvious in our own culture. We do not all enjoy shooting a six-gun or lassoing a pony, yet a foreigner noting the prominence of western themes in our entertainment media might think so.

The third approach, the study of child-rearing systems, can prove to be just as misleading. Shibutani deals extensively with this problem and ultimately asserts that specific child-rearing practices are related to personality development only insofar as they constitute manifestations of the mother toward the child. As far as Shibutani is concerned, the style of a mother's care is more important than the technique.[42] He is not alone in his assertion and cites studies by Brody (1956), Behrens (1954), and Wahl (1954) to support his view. To give an example from our own culture, most middle-class Americans try to instill independence, ambition, and nonviolence in their children. Why, then, are not all middle-class youths independent, ambitious, and nonviolent? The crucial factor is the difference in affective relationships in primary-group settings. At this point, it must be noted that the effect on personality of certain child-rearing practices reported by Kardiner, Mead, and Malinowski may well exist, but not to the extent supposed by their readers. Assertions of that type place far too much emphasis on early childhood and not enough on significant experiences occurring in adolescence and later life.[43]

The idea of the significant existence of a relatively stable, modal personality type within a society has a very limited application. In fact, the idea of a national character is often nothing other than a stereotype applied to nations and/or cultures. It must be noted that not all stereotypes are completely without foundation. The problem is the extent to which they are generalized. The idea of a national character assumes that a person has a certain type of personality as opposed to the personality of a member of a different ethnic group. The truth is, however, that different nationals may behave differently to accommodate their institutions but the range of personality types within all cultures is quite similar. In the case of primitive, homogenous societies such as those studied by Mead, there could be some truth in the idea of national character. These societies often take harsh, dedicated steps to repress natural impulses or instill certain attitudes in their children. When people accept the idea of national character, they should limit this concept to relatively isolated, taboo-ridden cultures and not generalize to modern, heterogeneous, industrialized nations.

D. A REVIEW

In this chapter we have observed the process of socialization. Starting with nonverbal responses in the human infant, social experiences increase in both complexity and frequency. Soon the developing child acquires knowledge of the system of verbal symbols we call language. Because of language, he is able to reflect on behavior, both past and present. With further sophistication, he develops comprehension of the future and abstract world in which he will eventually interact. Through the basic processes of classical and instrumental learning, greatly complicated and amplified by the superior physiology of the human brain, an individual finds himself living in a world of both physical and abstract reality. Through the treatment he receives, and thinks he receives, the personality of the individual is jelled by the primary and secondary groups with which he is associated. In contemporary society, there are important socializing variables which did not exist in the past. Mass media affect the development of the human in ways that are not fully assessed as yet. Nevertheless, the human is capable of socializing himself and, after a certain point, becomes the most important determinant of his own behavior. Through a process of developing reference groups and engaging in anticipatory socialization, an individual tries to make of himself that which he perceives as good. In the final analysis, each and every personality is a product of the unique experiences it has undergone. No nation produces a uniform character, but possesses a vast array of personalities.

The problem of this study is not the nature of the socialization process. We are more concerned with those whose socialization has somehow gone awry. What happens to them? Are they absorbed by their society, rejected by it or, in some way, resocialized by it? These are the questions to be dealt with in the following pages.

FOOTNOTES

1. Kimball Young, *Sociology: A Study of Society and Culture* (2nd ed.; New York: American Book Company, 1949), p. 63.
2. I. L. Child, "Socialization," in *The Handbook of Social Psychology*, ed. by G. Lindzey (Cambridge: Addison-Wesley Publishing Co., 1954) p. 655.
3. Paul B. Horton and Chester L. Hunt, *Sociology* (2nd ed.; New York: McGraw-Hill Book Company, 1964), p. 98.

4. Clare K. Nicholson, *Anthropology and Education*, Foundations of Education Series (Columbus: Charles E. Merrill Publishing Company, 1968), p. 77.
5. Joseph S. Roucek in *Dictionary of Sociology*, ed. by Henry Pratt Fairchild (Totowa: Littlefield, Adams & Co., 1968), p. 298.
6. Pitirim Sorokin, *Fads and Foibles in Modern Sociology* (Chicago: Henry Regnery Company, 1956), pp. 3-20.
7. George H. Mead, *On Social Psychology*, ed. by Anselm Strauss (Chicago: University of Chicago Press, 1964), pp. 199-246.
8. Tamotsu Shibutani, *Society and Personality* (Englewood Cliffs: Prentice-Hall, Inc., 1961), pp. 344-345.
9. Konrad Lorenz, *On Aggression* (New York: Harcourt, Brace and World, Inc., 1963); see Chapter V in particular.
10. Edward T. Hall, *The Silent Language* (Greenwich: Fawcett Publications, Inc., 1959); see Chapters 3, 9, and 10.
11. Leonard Broom and Phillip Selznick, *Sociology: A Text with Adapted Readings* (4th ed.; New York: Harper & Row, 1968), p. 96.
12. *loc. cit.*
13. James Deese, *The Psychology of Learning* (2nd ed.; New York: McGraw-Hill Book Company, Inc., 1958), pp. 8-9.
14. *loc. cit.*
15. Ernest R. Hilgard, *Introduction to Psychology* (3rd ed.; New York: Harcourt, Brace & World, Inc., 1962), p. 258.
16. Deese, *op. cit.*, p. 11.
17. Hilgard, *op. cit.*, pp. 259-260.
18. For a rather technical yet comprehensible discussion of language, see Roger Brown, *Social Psychology* (New York: The Free Press, 1965), Chapters 6-7.
19. Ernest G. Schachtel, *Metamorphosis* (New York: Basic Books, 1959), pp. 279-322.
20. Edward Sapir, "The Status of Linguistics as a Science," *Language*, V (1929), p. 209.
21. Charles H. Cooley, *Social Organization* (New York: Charles Scribner's Sons, 1909), pp. 23-24.
22. *loc. cit.*
23. Charles H. Cooley, *Human Nature and the Social Order* (New York: Shocken Books, Inc., 1964), p. 184.
24. *loc. cit.*
25. Mead, *op. cit.*, pp. 218-219.
26. David Riesman, *The Lonely Crowd* (New Haven: Yale University Press, 1961), pp. 109-140.
27. Robert K. Merton, "Social Structure and Anomie," *Social Theory and Social Structure* (New York: The Free Press, 1968), pp. 185-214.
28. The public has been made aware of the influence of the media. Remember the effects of the radio broadcast "Invasion from Mars" by Orson Welles. Peruse also Vance Packard, *The Hidden Persuaders* (New York: Pocket Books, 1958).
29. August Kerber and Wilfred Smith, eds., "The Functions of Mass Culture," in *Educational Issues in a Changing Society* (Detroit: Wayne State University Press, 1968), pp. 64-65.
30. Again, this is a primary function of the broadcasters and

advertisers codes of ethics.

31. Kerber and Smith, *op. cit.*, pp. 66-67.
32. Orville G. Brim, Jr., "Adult Socialization," in *Socialization and Society*, ed. by John Clausen (Boston: Little, Brown and Company, 1968), p. 184.
33. Rolf E. Muus, *Theories of Adolescence* (2nd ed.; New York: Random House, 1968), p. 50. Erikson thinks the adolescent is almost always at odds with his parents. This is not necessarily so.
34. E. Z. Friedenberg, *The Vanishing Adolescent* (Boston: Beacon Press, 1959), p. 13.
35. David Krech, Richard S. Crutchfield, and Egerton L. Ballachey, *Individual in Society* (New York: McGraw-Hill Book Company, Inc., 1962), p. 102.
36. It is here that the "self-fulfilling prophecy" is vital. For example, if treated as lazy, an individual might act it, leading to more of the same treatment.
37. Maurice Farber, "The Analysis of National Character," in *Personality and Social Systems*, ed. by Neil and William Smelser (New York: John Wiley and Sons, Inc., 1963), p. 81.
38. Alex Inkeles and Daniel Levinson, "National Character: The Study of Modal Personality and Sociocultural Systems," in Vol. II of *Handbook of Social Psychology*, ed. by Gardiner Lindzey (Reading: Addison-Wesley, Inc., 1954), p. 983.
39. *ibid.*, p. 85.
40. Inkeles and Levinson, *op. cit.*, p. 995.
41. *ibid.*, p. 996.
42. Shibutani, *op. cit.*, pp. 557-558.
43. Inkeles and Levinson, *op. cit.*, p. 998.

II. WHEN SOCIALIZATION "FAILS"

A. MISSING THE OBJECTIVE

1. Shortcomings

The manifest function of socialization is to develop a human being capable of coping with the daily requirements of social living. He must be able to communicate with other members of his society, live according to their norms, and procure food and shelter for himself and his family. Ideally individuals develop these abilities as they undergo the process of socialization. Actually, however, some do not. For various sociological and psychological reasons, socialization has not left them with the cultural tools required by society at large. Many individuals are unable to make their ideas known to their fellows. They cannot engage in true dialogue due to a failure to master word symbols. Others cannot conduct their activities without interfering with those of their neighbors. Still others find it difficult to provide the basic necessities of life for themselves. This leads to a basic question, "Have these individuals been socialized?" At first glance, it would appear that such individuals have not reaped the full benefits of the socialization process. To such a question, however, there are a myriad of possible answers. The following are two such alternates.

2. Alternate Considerations

a. The Relative Nature of Socialization. Although socialization is a universal process, it is a relative matter. Groups within a society may hold an abundance of mutual values yet remain distinct because they differ on one. Certain subcultures may choose to emphasize education as a method of acquiring wealth whereas others might emphasize the field of politics. The fact is that members of certain subcultures often acquire values and ideas which differ from those of others. In adhering to their particular values, they may be considered unsocialized by the society at large, yet they may be adequately socialized with reference to their particular subculture. To say that an individual is not socialized because he is not in accordance with the dominant culture may be more a value judgment than a statement of fact.

b. The Question of Enculturation. There is another approach to the question of socialization. Some anthropologists and sociologists consider a man to be socialized even if he is capable of meeting only the minimum requirements of social living. If he is able to communicate and interact to such a degree that he is able to survive as a social animal, then he is socialized. His behavior may fall short of the ideal norms of his own subculture but, nevertheless, he is a member of a society. Melville Herskovits invented the term "enculturation" to explain those members of society whose learned behavior approximates the ideal. These individuals have truly absorbed their total culture and participate fully in their society. They are "enculturated."[1]

3. The Methodological Question

Having discussed these relative and theoretical questions pertaining to socialization, attention must be focused on a methodological question. How can one best observe the products of socialization and more specifically, the failures of socialization? Rephrased, one might ask, "In what areas can the failures of socialization best be observed?" To answer this question, the methodological ideas of Emile Durkheim will be explored. Durkheim believed that sociology is the study of social facts, and that sociological facts can best be observed through the study of institutional behavior. Since he believed that human behavior is essentially a group phenomenon, it follows that social aggregates, or rather social institutions, should be the springboard of sociological investigation.[2] For the purposes of this study, we shall examine the failure of socialization in three institutional areas: education, criminolegal systems, and industry.[3]

4. Visible "Failures"

Educational failures are visible in many ways. There are numerous individuals in our society who have not acquired the symbolic processes and communicative abilities necessary for "effective" social living. The institution of education has a major responsibility in the socialization of societal members. During a period of twelve or thirteen years, the educational institution is charged with teaching the individual to read, write, perform mathematical operations, and comprehend a number of complex physical and biological processes. Many educators believe the institution should be even more active in developing the individual. John Childs, for example, considers the school to be a prime agent of social change and total cultural transmission.[4] While this concept will not be disputed here, let it suffice that education has the major responsibility of developing the verbal and cognitive abilities of its charges. Yet there are products of the educational institution who are unable to write a letter or read a newspaper. While others around them are enjoying a good book, they can only look at the pictures. Any conversation of which they are a part must entail a limited vocabulary since their word-symbol fund is not extensive. In the past, functional illiterates had been limited largely to high school dropouts. In recent years, however, more and more high school graduates fall into this category. Inadequate education becomes even more visible in a society where technical knowledge is prerequisite for an increasing number of jobs. Where an occupation requires an ability to manipulate verbal and mathematical symbols, these educational failures are inadequate. Education, however, is geared to develop more than grammatical and mathematical faculties. Education also attempts to teach the individual to live as a functional and nondestructive member of society. Those who fail to acquire these abilities are often visible in the criminolegal systems.

Whereas the educational institution serves more to nurture growth and productive activity, criminolegal systems function to arrest antisocial activity and restore it to acceptable behavior. Each time an individual breaks a criminal law, the dominant society identifies him as a result of the failure of socialization. At this point, he is associated with and subjected to the processes of the criminolegal systems. Certainly the initial instance of antisocial behavior (the breaking of a law) may be attributable to other social institutions. However, it is the rehabilitative nature of the criminolegal systems that we are most concerned with in this study. Theoretically, the criminolegal systems have been moving from a punitive approach toward lawbreakers to a rehabilitative one. This change, according to Karl Menninger, has long been needed.[5] Although he believes that the criminolegal systems will have a long way to go in this direction, the rehabilitative approach has become dominant. Nevertheless, a great number of adjudicated criminals are recidivists. Most have been subjected at one time or another to those rehabilitative processes at the disposal of the state: incarceration, probation, parole, half-way houses, group therapy, psychotherapy, etc. Notwithstanding institutional attempts, a great percentage of these individuals consistently fail to conduct themselves in accordance with the law. Certain social scientists believe the criminolegal system has also failed to perform its social duties by not adequately educating society about the dangers of drugs, promiscuity, and questionable associations. The institution, however, has responded to these criticisms and has increased its propaganda campaigns. It is within the criminolegal system, then, that failures of socialization can also be observed.

Finally, let us turn to industry. Socialization attempts to prepare the individual to take an active and productive role in his society. In the organic solidarity of contemporary America, the labor of one man contributes to the support of another, and vice versa. To maintain such a condition of equilibrium, each adult individual must somehow take part in the production of goods and services.[6] Yet, there are many individuals who are unable to acquire or maintain employment. Many go without work for years at a time and, if they find employment, maintain it only briefly. These failures of socialization are visible within the ranks of the hard-core unemployed, on the welfare roles, or as lifelong dependents. Socialization has failed to provide them with the values, attitudes, and abilities necessary for participation in the institution of industry.[7] As is the case with criminolegal systems, industrial failures are generally the result of inadequate preparation by other social institutions. It is in relation to the institutional area of industry, however, that they become highly visible.

Although the institutional areas of education, criminolegal systems, and industry have been treated as separate and distinct entities in the foregoing analysis, there is a high degree of overlap between them. The human products of inadequate socialization may be more visible in one institution than another, but the social etiology of their inadequacy may be quite the same. For example, a failure of the educational institution, the illiterate, might also become a failure in the industrial institution due to his relative inability to acquire or perform work. Such an individual, if motivated to gain money, may seek an alternative which would bring him into contact with the criminolegal systems. Thus, it must be understood that these institutional areas were distinguished from one another for analytic purposes only. In actuality, they are so related and mutually dependent that no single variable is unique to one institution.

5. The Responsibility of Society

One further caution is in order. The responsibility for inadequate socialization cannot be fixed on the individual alone. If the dominant society does not allow all of its members an equal access to the social institutions, then the society itself can be the cause of inadequate socialization. The denial of appropriate educational facilities to the American Negro in this country's history is the major cause of many educational "failures." Prejudice and discrimination on religious, racial, and ethnic bases have long been the cause of high crime rates and unemployment in various subcultures. Where this is the case, only the dominant society can be held responsible.

In the preceding pages, we have discussed the concept of "failure" in the socialization process. The use of the term is relative, not absolute. Since the dominant society controls accesss to the educational, political, and economic institutions of America, it is the dominant society which sets the norms by which all are expected to live and against which all are measured. An individual is considered to be poorly socialized by the dominant society when his behavior does not comply with its norms. These norms have a long and pervasive social history and exert a tremendous amount of influence in contemporary America. In order to better understand exactly what kind of behavior is expected by the dominant society, we turn to an historical investigation of those norms relating to education, criminolegal systems, and industry.

B. THE DEVELOPMENT OF INSTITUTIONAL NORMS

1. In Education

Education has long been valued in the dominant American culture. The roots of this affinity are older even than the Republic. In fact, education was considered important by the forefathers of our country long before they left the European continent. The Renaissance, or rebirth of learning, began in the 1200's and lasted through the Reformation of the 1500's. Many aspects of this movement had some influence on the development of contemporary American norms. The Renaissance replaced a religious point of view with a secular one, and made man rather than God the focal point of art, literature, and government. This "humanism," as it is often called, was based partly on the transfer of wealth and political power from the church to the laymen. It also included the revival of the ancient classical cultures of Greece and Rome. Classicism protested against the religious tone of education in the Middle Ages. Significant new inventions made rapid educational and learning progress possible. Printing vastly increased the availability of books to many segments of society, enabling people to think for themselves instead of accepting everything on the authority of scholars or priests. Advances in geography, exploration, and natural sciences, together with the revival of trade and the growth of cities, helped to develop the educative norms prominent in American society.[8] The movement which had the greatest effect on American education, however, was the Protestant Reformation. After the Act of Supremacy in 1534, a long and bitter struggle to establish a single religious belief took place in England. Such tribulations forged a powerful and closely-knit group, the Puritans, who began the first colonies in North America.[9] Education was of particular concern to the Puritans. Their movement was directed by university-trained divines and embraced primarily middle-class merchants and land-owning farmers who enjoyed the benefits of education in Elizabethan England. About 130 university alumni had come to New England by 1640. These men insisted their children have the advantages they themselves had. Consequently, parents in New England colonies were required to teach their children and servants to read or send them to a village school for that purpose.[10] Even more important, however, was the belief of the Protestant faith in a "priesthood of all believers." The colonial forefathers felt that an ability to read the Scriptures was mandatory if one wished to lead a faithful life. The "Old Deluder Satan Act" of Massachusetts Bay in 1647 is considered to be the first major school law because it was meant to ensure that all would know how to read.[11] Since that time, education has been considered valuable by the dominant American culture. There are other than religious foundations, however, for the norm of education.

The political creed of the United States is one of

democracy, a "government of the people." In theory, such a government depends for its stability on an intelligent and informed electorate. Dominant American reasoning holds that the ability to read is related to the ability to achieve an informed political judgment and to act accordingly. Partially the consequence of such a belief is the fact that literacy tests are required of voters in seventeen states of the union.[12] The twentieth century has also seen a tremendous expansion in the technical aspects of business and industry. In most cases, the ability to read and write is a necessary prerequisite to acquiring technological skills. In recognition of these conditions the American public has increasingly accepted the importance of at least a basic education. The establishment of education as "the American way" is most visible in a number of higher court decisions which sought to provide the optimum conditions under which education can flourish. Examples are: Stuart vs. School District No. 1 of Kalamazoo (Kalamazoo case) which authorized local boards of education to use tax money to operate secondary schools; Pierce vs. Society of the Sisters of the Holy Names of Jesus Christ (Oregon case) which stated that nonpublic schools are acceptable alternatives to public schools; and Cochran et al. vs. Louisiana State Board of Education et al. which established the "child benefit" theory. Certainly, some higher court decisions were interpreted in such a way as to hinder education in this country (Plessey vs. Ferguson, which led to segregation in the south) but such cases have since been reversed. Any investigation into the history of American education will reveal that, for the most part, the legal system has been highly supportive.[13] American legislators have been no less concerned about the progress of education in this country. From the federal ordinance of 1785 establishing land grant colleges, to the Elementary and Secondary Education Act, governments in this country have reinforced the norm of education.[14]

2. In Criminolegal Systems

It is much easier to trace the history of educational norms in this country than to explain the origin of our criminolegal systems. To this day, experts disagree on the sociocultural origins of the criminal laws prevalent in American society. In classical theory, the criminal law was regarded as having originated in torts, or the doing of "wrong" by individuals. As society progressed, the state considered a wrong committed against an individual as an affront to itself, thus prompting group reaction to such offenses. Another theory holds that criminal law origi- nated in the rational process of a unified society. When something is done which upsets the relationship between men, action is taken to restore matters to an equilibrium and to guard against its recurrence. Such action generally results in an edict or proscriptive statute. A third theory is that criminal law originated in and was crystallized by *mores.* Although customs usually develop without rational and concentrated analysis, once they are established infractions of such customs produce antagonistic reactions by the group. Still another theory holds that criminal law originated in the conflict of interests between groups. [15] Whichever group emerges victorious from such a conflict establishes criminal laws to protect itself from encroach- ment by the vanquished. In effect, the winners of the struggle decide who is to be involved in "violations" of the law. [16]

Whatever the normative origins of our criminolegal system, there are certain things about which experts generally agree. First and foremost, the person and his property are inviolable. Neither shall be harmed, removed, or otherwise molested without the adjudicated permission of a dominant institution. Secondly, no individual has done a criminal wrong if he has not violated an existing and explicitly recorded law. If certain behavior is repugnant to society, then it must be forbidden formally. Until such formal proscription is made, no criminal law has been violated and a man, at least in the technical sense, cannot be considered a criminal. There must also be a concurrence of act and intent. It is a basic principle of the Anglo-American criminolegal system, as well as other systems of justice, that neither an act alone nor an intent alone is sufficient to constitute a crime; the two must concur to establish criminal responsibility. "Act" is interpreted, however, to include a failure to act where there is a positive duty, as in the criminal negligence of a parent or physician.[17]

Once the law has been violated society must take some form of action if its proscriptions are to be considered binding. In theory, the treatment of a law-breaker in a society marked by mechanical solidarity will be different than in one marked by organic solidarity. The "collective conscience" of mechanical solidarity is all-powerful and intolerant of infractions of its norms. In such a society, social constraint is expressed most decisively in a severe and repressive criminal law. In the organic solidarity of contemporary America, however, the "collective conscience" is weakened by social heterogeneity. Thus, criminal law supported by repressive sanctions tends to be replaced by an emphasis on restitution for a crime rather than punishment for it.[18] It is for this reason that our criminolegal systems emphasize rehabilitation rather than punishment. This statement, however, must be qualified. There is often a difference between theory and practice, especially where the various social institutions are concerned. Although our criminolegal systems are guided by the theory of rehabilitation, this by no means ensures that their actions, in fact, are not highly punitive.

3. In Industry

The dominant norms of the American industrial institution are those of sacrifice, hard work, and material success. As with education there is a strong possibility that the origins of these norms can be traced to religion and the Reformation. Max Weber believed the spirit of capitalism, and the economic and industrial ideas which go with it, to be a result of the Protestant ethic. The Protestant ethic does not sanction acquisitiveness and hard work directly but stresses salvation. In its Calvinist form, salvation is presumed to depend on predestination. God has predetermined those who will be saved. Therefore, one can do nothing to achieve salvation. However, since salvation is the focus of a person's religious life, he is necessarily interested in knowing whether he is among the chosen. Success in one's secular or worldly calling is believed to be an almost infallible indication of being among those of God's children selected for salvation.[19] Thus, one who works hard and accumulates property and wealth is considered to be a "moral" man, one who is proving that he is worthy of leading "the good life."[20] There are those who might argue that the Protestant ethic was far more popular with our forefathers than with contemporary generations. Literary and sociological investigations have shown, however, that this is not necessarily so. The tremendous popularity of Horatio Alger's works around the turn of the century, and even today, indicates that the norm of hard work leading to material success is a powerful influence on American life. The "rags to riches" sagas of Alger's literary heroes have inspired and thrilled many readers and have become part of the "American way." Certainly Alger's writings have been criticized by intellectuals and historians, but this criticism has never penetrated the thinking of most Americans.[21] A more contemporary writer has described in detail the Protestant ethic and its dominance in American life. William H. Whyte believes the pursuit of individual salvation through hard work, thrift, and competitive struggle is at the heart of American achievement. Although he concedes that many people will deny that the Protestant ethic holds true for them, he still believes this norm predominates in American life.[22]

The preceding discussion concerning the normative history of education, criminolegal systems, and industry needs to be brought into perspective. First, the statements contained therein apply to the dominant culture only. There are many subcultures for whom the above generalizations do not apply. These subcultures, however, may have a unique normative history as old and as integrative as has the dominant culture. Unfortunately, this research is too limited to treat them at length. Second, as has been stated before, there is a tremendous degree of overlap in the normative histories explored thus far. They have been separated for purposes of analysis only. To consider them as separate phenomena in actual practice would be a gross theoretical and methodological error. Finally, the normative requirements of education, criminolegal systems, and industry can only be discussed on a qualitative basis. It is impossible to say that education requires ten years of course work with a "C" average or that industry requires the expenditure of a certain amount of energy per hour five days a week. To attempt to put a quantitative definition in the framework of a norm is absurd, if not impossible. Suffice it to say that the members of a dominant society have internalized guidelines by which infractions of a norm can be measured. Since society is dynamic, these guidelines can change. They do not often change so rapidly, however, that complete consensus is lost. The norms of the dominant society still maintain that a man is expected to read and write, live in accordance with the law, and provide for himself and his family. Socialization is the means by which a man acquires these values, attitudes, and abilities. As has been pointed out before, however, many individuals fail to acquire the prerequisites for living according to the norms of the dominant society. Where this is the case, and where a society perceives it to be so, societal dissonance exists.

C. SOCIETAL DISSONANCE

1. Ideal vs. Real Behavior

In the preceding section, the normative expectations of the educational, criminolegal, and industrial institutions were discussed. It has also been observed that many individuals within a society are unable to meet these behavioral expectations. This discrepancy may be discussed in terms of "ideal" versus "real" behavior. The dominant society operates according to a set of established "ideal" norms. This means that members of a society are expected to be able to communicate effectively in both a written and spoken manner, live without breaking the laws of the dominant society and, finally, to support one's self and family. Yet, in reality, many fall short of these behavioral requirements or, at least, the dominant society perceives their actions to be inadequate. This discrepancy between "ideal" behavior and perceived "real" behavior leads to a state of societal dissonance.[23]

2. Restoration of Equilibrium

The concept of societal dissonance can best be understood by examining the social theories of Vilfredo Pareto. For Pareto, society is a system in a state of equilibrium. There exist within every society certain forces which maintain the form or condition which the society has achieved or which guarantee even and uninterrupted change; in the latter case the equilibrium is dynamic. There is an important corollary to this principle: If the social system is subjected to pressures from outward forces of moderate intensity, inner forces will push toward the restoration of equilibrium, returning the society to its undisturbed state. These inner forces consist primarily of the sentiment of revulsion against anything which disturbs the inner equilibrium.[24] Applying these theories to the effects of inadequate socialization on society, let us consider the poorly educated, criminal, or chronic unemployed as pressures because they are unable to play the integral roles necessary for equilibrium of the social system. The existence of such individuals disrupts a society in proportion to their numbers, leading to a state of societal dissonance. The dominant society then works to restore consonance (equilibrium) by attempting to modify behavior until it conforms with dominant norms. A basic question, and the focus of this research, is "How does a society work to restore equilibrium?" Other relevant queries are "What action does a society take to bring behavior into conformity?", "What processes are involved in this action?", and "How successful is society at altering behavior?" To explore possible answers to some of these questions, let us turn to Chapter III, the Nature of Resocialization.

FOOTNOTES

1. See Melville J. Herskovits, *Man and His Works* (New York: Alfred A. Knopf, 1948).
2. Nicholas T. Timasheff, *Sociological Theory: Its Nature and Growth* (3rd ed.; New York: Random House, 1967), p. 110.
3. It is noted that these social institutions are not as strictly defined or differentiated as they may be by institutional sociologists. For the purposes of this study, however, they are being defined as social institutions and, as such, will be employed as areas of investigation.
4. See John Childs, *Education and Morals* (New York: Appleton-Century Crofts, Inc., 1950).
5. See Karl Menninger, *The Crime of Punishment* (New York: The Viking Press, 1966).
6. This principle can be traced back to Emile Durkheim, *Division of Labor in Society*, trans. by George Simpson (Glencoe, Illinois: The Free Press, 1947). Durkheim's original work, in French, appeared in 1893.
7. Industry, as it is designated herein, refers to numerous aspects of economic endeavor and encompasses primary, secondary, and tertiary activities.
8. John D. Pulliam, *History of Education in America,* Foundation of Education Series (Columbus: Charles E. Merrill Publishing Co., 1968), pp. 5-6.
9. *ibid,* p. 6.
10. Samuel E. Morison and Henry S. Commager, Vol. I of *The Growth of the American Republic* (5th ed.; New York: Oxford University Press, 1962), p. 63.
11. Pulliam, *op. cit.,* p. 5.
12. Marian D. Irish and James W. Prothro, *The Politics of American Democracy* (2nd ed.; Englewood Cliffs: Prentice-Hall, Inc., 1959), pp. 362-3.
13. For a review of legal milestones in educational history, see Roald R. Campbell, Luvern L. Cunningham, and Roderick F. McPhee, *The Organization and Control of American Schools* (Columbus: Charles E. Merrill Publishing Company, 1965), pp. 10-14.
14. *ibid.,* pp. 20-46.
15. Edwin H. Sutherland and Donald R. Cressey, *Principles of Criminology* (7th ed.; New York: J. B. Lippincott Company, 1966), pp. 9-11.
16. George B. Vold, *Theoretical Criminology* (New York: Oxford University Press, 1958), pp. 208-209.
17. Paul W. Tappan, *Crime, Justice, and Correction* (New York: McGraw-Hill Book Company, Inc., 1960), p. 10.
18. For a more detailed exploration of this notion, first advanced by Durkheim, see Timasheff, *op. cit.,* pp. 112-113.
19. *ibid.,* p. 173.
20. Mere wealth is not sufficient to be among the "chosen." One must have acquired this wealth through disciplined, orderly, and legal endeavor.

21. R. Richard Wohl, "The Rags to Riches Story," in *Class, Status and Power*, ed. by Reinhard Bendix and Seymore M. Lipset (2nd ed.; New York: The Free Press, 1966), pp. 501-506.
22. William H. Whyte, Jr., *The Organization Man* (New York: Simon and Schuster, Inc., 1956), pp. 3-15.
23. For an application of this principle on a psychological level, see Ross Stagner, *Psychology of Personality* (3rd ed.; New York: McGraw-Hill Book Company, Inc., 1961), p. 209.
24. Timasheff, *op. cit.*, pp. 162-163.

III. THE NATURE OF RESOCIALIZATION

A. RESOCIALIZATION AS A PROCESS

1. Resocialization Defined

In order to restore social consonance, or the compatibility of ideal and real behavior, a society must take action which affects behavior on an individual basis. To this end, the dominant institutions plan and execute dynamic programs aimed at the "resocialization" of certain members of society. For the purposes of this book, resocialization is defined in the following manner:

> Resocialization is that process wherein an individual, defined as inadequate according to the norms of a dominant institution(s), is subjected to a dynamic program of behavior intervention aimed at instilling and/or rejuvenating those values, attitudes, and abilities which would allow him to function according to the norms of said dominant institution(s).

As discussed in the previous chapter, members of the dominant society internalize a set of behavioral standards according to which individuals are expected to comply. When certain individuals do not perform according to these standards, they become visible in the institutional areas of education, criminolegal systems, and industry. In order to restore society to a state of consonance, the dominant society subjects them, by force or persuasion, to dynamic programs of behavior intervention aimed at altering their values, attitudes, and abilities until they conform to the norms of the dominant institutions.[1] These programs can be defined as a process of resocialization.

39

2. A Dynamic Model of Resocialization

In order to better clarify the process of resocialization, perhaps a visual model would be appropriate. Figure 3 shows one of several possible analogous models suitable for this purpose.

The overlapping circles designating the state of society before resocialization indicate a greater degree of societal dissonance than consonance. The reason for this degree of dissonance can be attributed to the gap between real and ideal behavior, as indicated by the double arrow at the top of the diagram. Schematically, there would be an inverse relationship between the behavior gap and the degree of

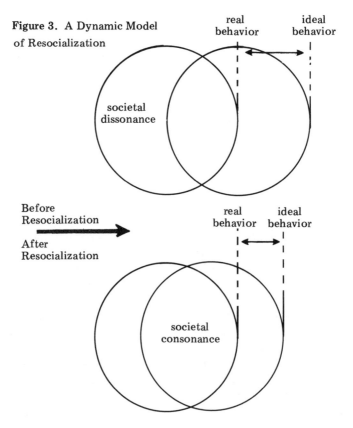

Figure 3. A Dynamic Model of Resocialization

societal consonance. In order to increase consonance, society must institute dynamic programs aimed at bringing real behavior closer to ideal. The institution of such programs is represented by the large arrow at the left of the diagram. The direction of the arrow indicates that the circle on the left would begin to merge with the one on the right. This would serve to reduce the gap between real and ideal behavior, thus increasing the degree of societal consonance. This diagram, of course, oversimplifies the totality of processes involved in resocialization and assumes that the circle moves in only one direction. Since many forms of collective action are composed of a variety of conflicting forces, progress is seldom continuous or direct. We must interpret Figure 3 as merely a theoretical tool to be employed in better understanding, rather than defining, the process of resocialization.

3. Forms of Resocialization

a. *Compensatory Education.* Since we are primarily concerned with behavior in education, criminolegal systems, and industry, discussion will be limited to resocialization programs pertaining to these institutions. When the socialization process fails to develop the capacity or desire to read, write, and effectively communicate with others, the educational institution designs a program of resocialization which might be termed "compensatory." More specifically, compensatory education refers to "education programs, practices, techniques, and projects designed to overcome the deficiencies of children from culturally disadvantaged homes and to enable them to fulfill the fundamental purposes of education."[2] An attempt is made to have the subject value education and approach it with a positive attitude. Compensatory education is a wide-ranging form of resocialization which divides itself into many and varied approaches, depending on the assessed needs of the individual. A more thorough and detailed analysis of compensatory education and its theories will be presented in Chapter IV.

b. Criminal Rehabilitation. The socialization process is concerned with developing an individual capable of compatible living. He is proscribed from interfering with the rights and property of others and expected to live according to the norms of the dominant society. When the individual violates these norms, the criminolegal systems subject him to a form of resocialization termed "criminal rehabilitation." In the rehabilitation process, the individual is, theoretically, exposed to a set of conditions which lead him to realize that behavior conforming to the dominant norms brings more emotional and material rewards than behavior opposing the dominant norms. As is the case with compensatory education, criminal rehabilitation encompasses a variety of theories and practices adapted to individual needs. Chapter V contains a more detailed analysis of resocialization in criminal rehabilitation.

c. Training for the "Hard-Core" Unemployed. In contemporary American society, each individual is expected to play a productive and complementary role in the industrial arena. For many individuals, however, the normal socialization process has proven inadequate in instilling values, attitudes, and abilities necessary for maintaining sufficient and continuous employment. These individuals are often termed "hard-core unemployed" and become the targets of resocialization programs aimed at teaching them the skills and attitudes required by the industrial institution. Training programs will vary according to institutional needs and economic conditions and often operate along diverse theoretical lines. Particulars concerning the theories and efficacy of these programs are presented in Chapter VI.

Since counseling and psychotherapy are used in all forms of resocialization, their nature and efficacy will be considered in Chapter VII. As will also be noted in pursuant chapters, most resocialization programs are highly interrelated. Improvement in one institutional area is usually accompanied by improvement in another. This serves to emphasize a point made earlier, that the social etiology of inadequacy can often be traced to a common source.

B. SOCIALIZATION VERSUS RESOCIALIZATION

1. A Table of Differences

The socialization process functions to develop an individual who is capable of coping with the requirements and pressures of everyday living. For reasons yet to be discussed, however, many individuals who fail to acquire these necessary values, attitudes, and abilities become visible in the areas of education, criminolegal systems, and industry. Dominant society attempts to resocialize them, essentially by providing them with stimuli favorable to learning to live according to dominant norms; to behave according to the ideal. Viewed in this manner, resocialization might seem to be nothing more than a repetition of certain parts of the original process of socialization. This assumption, however, is quite misleading and leads to an oversimplification of both the theory and practice of resocialization. In order to clarify the distinction between socialization and resocialization, basic differences will be examined as depicted in Table 1.

Before beginning the analysis, however, a precaution must be noted. Whenever social scientists attempt to classify or quantify human behavior, they expose themselves to a methodological problem. Most data regarding human beings are continuous rather than discrete, thus making any form of categorization questionable. In Table 1, human behavior has been dichotomized and placed under various rubrics. While this is easy to do on paper, it is impossible to generalize to actual social activity. Furthermore, there is a great deal of overlap between one form of behavior and another, thus making any finite distinction even more questionable. Nevertheless, the use of categories seems important in depicting human behavior if only to provide a basis for conceptualization. Let us consider Table 1 as an ideal, or modal categorization, meant only to show differences rather than to provide finite definitions.

TABLE 1
Socialization vs. Resocialization

	SELF		AGENT	
	Socialization	Resocialization	Socialization	Resocialization
Who?	Tabula Rasa	Accumulated Experiences	Primary Group	Secondary Group
What?	Develop	Alter	Guide	Redirect
How?	Dependent	Independent	Affective	Disaffective
Why?	Natural Process	Comply	Natural Process	Restore Equilibrium
When?	Continuous	Sporadic	Continuous	Sporadic
Where?	Natural Setting	Artificial Setting	Natural Setting	Artificial Setting

2. Interpretations

Table 1 contains six basic questions about socialization and resocialization as considered from two points of view: that of the agent and that of the self. For our purposes, we shall consider the agent as the source of social experience and direction; the mentor. The self is the recipient, the object of both socialization and resocialization processes. In answer to the first question, Who?, we see that the primary group is active in the socialization process whereas in resocialization the secondary group is the primary agent. The self during resocialization consists of accumulated experiences, whereas in socialization it is considered a tabula rasa during the incipient stages. In resocialization, the individual is often older and has acquired more experiences. Clearly, there are major differences in the parties involved in socialization and resocialization. Whereas a family may try to teach a young, impressionable child the importance of respecting the rights of others during the socialization process, resocialization agents of the criminolegal systems are often charged with the responsibility of convincing a fully-grown adult that his behavioral pattern is in need of revision. This leads to another question. What occurs during the processes of socialization and resocialization? During socialization, the agent's primary function is to guide the formation of the self's personality. The self's only responsibility is to develop and to mature. During resocialization, however, the function of the agent is often to redirect the individual's efforts. The individual, or the self, is not just expected to develop but to alter previously learned behavior patterns. In socialization, the self's primary group guides him in the acquisition of, for example, work habits acceptable to the dominant industrial institution. During resocialization, however, the agent redirects behavior and expects the self to alter inadequate work habits so that they meet institutional requirements. How this is done constitutes a third question. The agent in socialization generally relies on the strength of an affective relationship, one theoretically composed of personal attachment to the self who, because of his age and economic standing, is dependent on the agent. In resocialization, the agent is merely didactic and impersonal. The self, in response, is less dependent and may even be resentful, especially since he is aware that the agent of the educational institution may have been the very one who defined him as inadequate in the first place.

The reason the self is subjected to socialization and resocialization presents another difference between the two processes. The agent socializes the self as a natural concomitant to social living. During resocialization, the agent is attempting to restore equilibrium to society by getting the self to comply with ideal normative requirements. The agent in socialization is acting; the agent in resocialization is reacting. The timetable according to which all of this occurs is also a factor distinguishing socialization from resocialization. During socialization, the agent and self interact on a continuous basis. Life itself is the classroom. During resocialization, the agent and self interact only sporadically and for brief periods of time. A self who develops a pattern of behavior opposed to the norms of a dominant institution has done so over a period of time often as long as the entire process of socialization. When an attempt to resocialize him is made by the agents of, for example, the criminolegal systems, it is on a sporadic basis. An adjudicated criminal may be incarcerated for brief periods of time during his career in an attempt to resocialize him. The original socialization process, on the other hand, subjected him to continuous and extensive indoctrination from the day he was born.

Socialization and resocialization also occur in different settings. During socialization, both agent and self interact in a natural setting. They are subjected to and partake in most activities which constitute the social system. During resocialization, both agent and self find themselves in an artificial setting. Each knows they have been brought together under "laboratory" conditions which may have internal validity but very little external validity. The inmate in a penal institution is expected to acquire acceptable patterns of behavior taught him while behind walls. Should he be released to again partake in societal living, much of what he may have learned will either be inapplicable or unsuitable.

The above dichotomies between socialization and resocialization, agent and self, are only theoretical in nature. Dichotomization suggests that there are clear-cut lines where socialization ends and resocialization begins or that the agent and self are totally distinct entities. This is not so. Since the process of socialization never really ends, resocialization can be considered part of an individual's socialization. Furthermore, an individual can be both an agent of socialization and the recipient self. A father may be engaged in socializing his children while, at the same time, he is partaking in a resocialization program aimed at altering his behavior.

Certainly, the generalizations relating to Table 1 cannot be applied to each and every resocialization program. For example, the resocialization agent does not necessarily maintain a disaffective relationship with a self. Many teachers in compensatory education programs have a profound and vital concern for their charges and are able to evoke a considerable amount of interest and affection in them. Resocialization is not solely in the realm of a secondary group. Many families have themselves identified a member to be in need of resocialization and made concerted efforts to alter or redirect his behavior. Thus, the information contained in Table 1 is meant only to organize and identify certain aspects of socialization and resocialization, not to define basically inseparable phenomena. Furthermore, the discussion of the differences between socialization and resocialization is of a very superficial nature. The effects of affective interaction versus disaffective interaction were not explored in detail, nor were the distinctions between primary and secondary activities highlighted. These omissions are not the result of oversight but were made in deference to the organization and presentation of this research. In later chapters, the human processes involved in various resocialization programs will be more fully explored.

C. RESOCIALIZATION IN CONTEMPORARY SOCIETY

1. History and Scope of Resocialization

Resocialization in its various forms has existed in this country for some time, although not to a great extent. Around the turn of the century, little was done to resocialize those individuals judged by the dominant institutions as inadequate. In education, they were merely dropped from school. If they committed a crime, they were simply incarcerated. When unable to maintain employment, they were often left to fend for themselves. This finalistic approach to the problem of inadequate socialization seems to have persisted until the 1930's, when universal suffrage and the Great Depression combined to revive an interest in the human being as an individual. Since that time, federal and state governments have taken a greater interest in the welfare of the citizenry. Labor laws, social security, civil rights acts, and special action grants have focused attention on the importance of the individual to society. This concern has extended to those formerly on the margins. Whenever possible, boards of education establish compensatory education programs and hire teachers especially trained for resocialization. The criminolegal systems have tried to abandon their traditionally punitive philosophy and constantly engage in rehabilitative experiments such as half-way houses, group therapy, and work-release programs. In industry, corporation executives have found the establishment of training programs for the hard-core unemployed to be very helpful to their relations with the government and the community. In short, resocialization is in vogue. Nearly every social institution has designed and implemented at least one resocialization program. Although such programs may be first to be cancelled when funds are low, they are often the first to be re-established when economic conditions are favorable. Those institutions which do not partake in resocialization programs are considered archaic or unenlightened and soon respond to public pressure to involve themselves. These resocialization programs have been examined, evaluated, and judged, generally by those who direct them. Although conflicting results have been reported, many students of human behavior insist that individuals can be and are being resocialized.

2. Analysis of Current Programs

The focus of our research is to examine in detail the various forms of resocialization taking place in contemporary society. Resocialization as it applies to education, criminolegal systems, and industry will be discussed. Counseling and psychotherapy will also be investigated. To give a broader perspective to the material, the various psychological and sociological theories regarding the etiology of inadequate socialization are included. Data concerning the theories and effectiveness of these programs will also be presented in an attempt to provide objective bases for program evaluation. Up to this point, discussion of resocialization in the institutional areas of education, criminolegal systems, and industry has been on a superficial basis. In succeeding chapters, however, this situation will be rectified. The importance of this type of research should not be underestimated. The amount of money and time involved in the numerous resocialization programs, as well as the human nature of their goals, indicate a vital need for a thorough and objective analysis of resocialization in contemporary society.

FOOTNOTES

1. A value is a personal estimate of the quality of a situation. An attitude is a readiness to respond in a certain way when the appropriate situation occurs; a mental set. An ability is a proficiency in any type of general or specific behavior. Phillip L. Harriman, *Handbook of Psychological Terms* (Totowa: Littlefield, Adams and Co., 1968), pp. 211, 17, 1 respectively.
2. John M. Beck and Richard W. Saxe, *Teaching the Culturally Disadvantaged Pupil* (Springfield: Bannerstone House, 1965), p. 43.

IV. RESOCIALIZATION IN EDUCATION: COMPENSATORY EDUCATION

A. NATURE AND EXTENT OF THE PROBLEM

1. The Culturally Disadvantaged Underachiever

Those who are subjected to programs of compensatory education tend to have a number of common characteristics. They are often at the bottom of American society in terms of income and generally reside in urban ghetto areas. They are subject to social and economic discrimination at the hands of the majority of society and, in racial and ethnic terms, are about evenly divided between whites and nonwhites. Many are Negroes from the rural south, whites from the rural south, urban dwellers, Puerto Ricans, Mexicans, Indians, and European immigrants with a rural background.[1] For one reason or another, they are limited in cultural experiences and have a relatively narrow perspective of the world in which they live. Their opportunities and choices are highly restricted and their future generally promises to be as bleak as their present and past. They are often referred to as "slow learners" and do not display a marked verbal-symbolic ability in the educational setting. More specifically, they demonstrate a short attention span, little self-confidence, apathy to schoolwork, low power of retention and memory, inability to do abstract thinking, and a failure to transfer ideas.[2] A more operational definition would state that they perform at roughly the 75 to 90 I.Q. level despite indications of higher capabilities. They achieve below their inferred ability because of varied maturation rates, environmental variables, test limitations, or possible multiple factors.[3]

The most crucial factor in the placement of a student in a compensatory education program is his degree of "school preparedness." Failure to provide the newly-born or infant child with sufficient sensory stimulation can have serious effects on later cognitive functioning. This failure is most visible in the lower classes. Preverbal and verbal deprivation also occurs in the more prosperous classes. Thus, certain of the middle class may be placed in, or be in need of, compensatory education.[4] The problem of defining those needing compensatory education is complicated by the number of writers on the subject. The terms "culturally deprived," "deprived," "underprivileged," "disadvantaged," and "slow learner" are often used interchangeably. For the purposes of this study, the subjects of compensatory education programs will be defined as "culturally disadvantaged underachievers." They are culturally disadvantaged because they are symbolically and experientially deprived and, because of this deprivation, they underachieve.

Having thus defined the problem for compensatory education, an understanding of the extent of the problem is in order. Difficulty with reading seems to be a major characteristic of the culturally deprived underachiever. A recent Harris survey indicated that 18.5 million Americans aged 16 and older lack the reading ability to get along in contemporary society without help.[5] Considering the fact that this survey included only that proportion of the population aged 16 and over, the problem seems quite extensive. Frank Riessman has noted that one out of ten children in the fourteen largest cities of the United States was "culturally deprived" in 1950. By 1960, he claimed this figure had risen to one in three and estimated that in 1970 the figure would be one out of two.[6]

For the nation as a whole, including adults, Fantini and Weinstein estimate that 77 million Americans are considered "deprived."[7] A somewhat more modest estimate was made by Abraham, who wrote: "Agreement is fairly general that these children constitute 15 to 20 percent of our school population . . ."[8] Havighurst places the number of socially disadvantaged children at about 15 percent of the child population. For major cities, however, he estimates that 30 percent fall into the socially disadvantaged category.[9]

Accurate and compatible statistics are not as important to this research as is the need to recognize that there is a problem and that this problem is extensive. During the process of socialization, and within the institution of education, a significant proportion of children are inadequately socialized. Their desire and/or ability to communicate with the wider (or dominant) society is rather limited, as is their perception of the alternatives available in life. The dominant society, however, makes an effort to identify culturally disadvantaged underachievers and to place them in a compensatory education program. The history and magnitude of this effort are the next topics of investigation.

2. History and Scope of Compensatory Education

Although the term "compensatory education" is relatively new, the notion is not. At least as far back as the Civil War, various social institutions had realized the need of certain citizens for increased experience and opportunity. During the period of Reconstruction, the Freedmen's Bureau and other organizations became active in the development of educational facilities for former slaves. Once the northern occupation had ended, however, compensatory education suffered a temporary setback. Despite the change in the popular mood, educational concern for the disadvantaged, still primarily Negroes, continued. Although their personal and educational philosophies differed, men such as Booker T. Washington and W. E. B. DuBois did a great deal for the education of the culturally disadvantaged underachiever.[10]

The European immigrations beginning around 1880 brought a new population of disadvantaged Caucasians. The major problems of these immigrants and their children seems to have been born of language differences. Nevertheless, the educational institution, having been made accessible to all, began to realize that many of its students were in need of help. The social concern born of the depression and the movement toward universal suffrage meant a great deal to the future of compensatory education for the culturally deprived. Soon after World War II, serious national attention began to be given to the problems of education for the disadvantaged. Certain pilot projects date back to the mid-forties when New York City's Harlem Project was initiated. Also, ground-breaking work had begun with Mexican-American and American Indian children in New Mexico. Probably the most important model for subsequent compensatory education programs was the Higher Horizons Program, which was formulated in the New York City Public School System in 1956.[11] Other cities around the nation had experimented with various forms of compensatory education by that time, and many were soon to make compensatory education a regular part of the school budget.[12]

A national conference called by the U. S. Office of Education in 1961 spotlighted the need for the establishment of special programs to re-educate the culturally deprived. By 1963, many of the 64 cities represented at the 1961 conference were doing something about the problem. The government demonstrated its concern for compensatory education by passing the Economic Opportunity Act of 1964. This measure allocated $280 million to combat poverty, of which 60 percent was earmarked for educational projects.[13] Next came the Elementary and Secondary Education Act of 1965. Under it, Title I provided financial assistance (approximately $1,060,000,000) for special educational programs in areas having high concentrations of children of low-income families.[14] Two other federal programs have been heavily funded and widely distributed. Upward Bound, which began in 1966, was designed to give precollege tutoring to disadvantaged high school students who, if left alone, would probably not even consider college. Across the U. S., nearly 300 colleges offer Upward Bound programs and about 23,000 high school students are currently taking part in them.[15] Project Headstart, designed to broaden the experience and verbal ability of disadvantaged preschool children, began operating in 1965 with more than a half-million children enrolled. Roughly the same number are currently participating with a cost to the federal government of $350 million.[16]

Clearly, the idea of compensatory education for the culturally deprived underachiever has become increasingly popular in this country. As evidence of its abrupt rise to popularity, one survey indicated that for the 76 programs for which starting dates were available, 93 percent were begun since 1960 and 43 percent just since 1963.[17] Certainly the programs mentioned in the preceding pages are by no means all-inclusive. Each state in the union and numerous branches and departments of the federal government operate a variety of compensatory education programs. In fact, it is quite probable that, due to the multitude of agencies and programs involved, the exact number of participants and dollars spent in compensatory education remains unknown. Although specific statistics may be difficult to provide, most compensatory education programs operate on the basis of mutually shared theories of the etiology and treatment of learning disability. The major theories relating to compensatory education will be reviewed in the next section.

B. THEORIES ON THE ETIOLOGY AND TREATMENT OF LEARNING DISABILITY

1. Physiological

The causes of underachievement and learning disability can be traced to numerous sources. One such source is the human body itself. Although all men may be born "spiritually equal," they are not all physically equal. The concept of evolution, which assumes the survival of those best fit to adapt to their environment, suggests a strong hereditary component in the differences not only between but among species. If one accepts the proposition that an offspring inherits the traits of his parents, intelligence might be considered an inheritable trait. If intelligence is inherited, it is because the brighter person inherits a nervous system that is superior to the one inherited by the less bright person.[18]   This by no means implies, however, that an individual's level of intelligence is set at birth and cannot be altered. Quite the contrary, it is believed that the level of intelligence of any given individual is subject to change, given certain socio-psychological experiences. [19] Nevertheless, the human body places limitations on just how much can be learned. If one's nervous system is characterized by poor neural connections, distorted or atrophic lobal growth, or any number of subnormal physiological characteristics, learning can be impaired. The electrochemical functions of the brain require a given physiological structure if learning is to be optimized.

Although most scientists seem to agree that intelligence (herein used as the capacity to learn) is inherited, few have qualified their propositions along racial lines. One educational psychologist at Berkeley, however, has proposed a theory which states that the different races, by virtue of inheritance, have different levels of intelligence. In essence, Arthur Jensen believes that the Negro is less capable than the Caucasian of a type of learning he calls cognitive. Cognitive learning consists of the abstract usage of concepts and ideas. Due to the "wiring pattern" of his brain, the Negro is less able to employ abstract conceptualization. On the other hand, according to Jensen's theory, the Negro is quite capable of associative learning. Essentially, associative learning is rote memorization. If this be true the nation's leaders should recognize this truth and make appropriate changes in our educational system in order to ensure that everyone receives the optimum type of learning the structure of his brain will allow. [20] However, at this time Jensen's theory has not been substantiated.

Physiological conditions adverse to learning can be traced to other than genetic factors. There are several prenatal and adolescent infirmities which can lead to permanent learning disability. For example, numerous children become retarded each year when measles turn into encephalitis. Any disease or glandular disorder, not necessarily determined by the genetic structure of the parents, can have grave consequences for the susceptible, developing, human infant. Fortunately, medical research has made considerable progress in recent years. Knowledge about the importance of prenatal care has been greatly disseminated throughout the population. The benefits of prevention, medication, diet, and surgery have reduced the number of children who develop learning disabilities unnecessarily.

Still other factors related to human physiology can lead to learning disability. Although their effects may not be as long-lasting or irreversible as genetic structure and disease, they merit investigation. A considerable number of children report for school every day with physical problems which, although not affecting brain structure, seriously deter learning. Some children have hearing defects which prevent them from fully participating in the aural phases of learning. Their poor performance is more related to an unfamiliarity with subject material than to any inherited trait. Others attend school with poor vision which, left uncorrected, prevents them from taking full advantage of reading material or blackboard illustrations. In many parts of the United States, poor health conditions related to poverty further contribute to learning disability. There is ample evidence that impoverished children often come to school undernourished, inadequately clothed, without sufficient sleep (partly because of overcrowded dwellings) and with untreated physical ills of an often acute and painful nature, such as a toothache.[21] Certainly children in such a physiological state cannot be expected to maintain the attention and interest in school necessary for learning. Given human nature, it is only natural that the greater part of their thinking would be directed toward the need to feed themselves or alleviate their pain.

Situations such as those just described relate directly to sociological and psychological theories of learning disability. Since these two scholarly fields so often overlap, they will be considered together in the next section along with theories on how to improve the situations described. The thoughts of selected experts in the field of educating the culturally disadvantaged underachiever will be examined. Since a complete review of the totality of their theories would be too voluminous, only major tenets will be presented.

2. Sociological and Psychological

A large number of educators believe that the major causes of learning disability can be attributed to the social surroundings of the culturally disadvantaged. The roots of the problem can be traced to early childhood and adolescent experiences in homes which do not transmit the cultural patterns necessary for the types of learning characteristic of the schools and the larger society. Many of the culturally disadvantaged underachievers come from homes in which adults have a minimal level of education. Poverty, large family size, broken homes, discrimination, slum conditions, and high crime rates further complicate the picture. Thus, according to Bloom et al., socio-economic conditions are closely related to learning disability and must become a subject of analysis.[22] Since the educational system in America today is one of age groupings, Bloom examines the problems of the culturally deprived in chronological order. As did Wolf and Wolf, he noted that many children attend school in poor physiological condition. As a first step in attacking the causes of learning disability, Bloom et al. recommend that each child be assured of an adequate breakfast, frequent physical examinations and appropriate medical care. In order to prevent any humiliation due to lack of necessary clothing, Bloom further recommends that each child be guaranteed appropriate garments.[23]

In discussing the early experiences of school children, Bloom points out that all do not begin their first day of school adequately prepared to learn. Beginning very early, the child perceives many aspects of the world around him. Through vision, hearing, touch, and taste, a child's perception broadens in proportion to the range of stimuli available to him. Whereas a typical middle-class home provides the child with a wide variety of stimuli, the range of perceptual experiences is often limited in the home of the culturally deprived. Such is the case with language as well. In culturally deprived homes, parents are less likely to expose a developing child to a wide variety of word-symbols. Physical or expressive gestures often constitute a large part of the communication in such families, thus preventing the child from extending and developing his speech. In many such homes the child is not encouraged to ask questions or require explanations. Such an approach to the naturally inquisitive child can discourage any desire for subsequent learning or "learning for its own sake." The early childhood experiences become even more crucial if one accepts the belief that all later learning is influenced by the very basic learning which has taken place by the age of five or six.[24]

In order to compensate for such experiential inequalities, Bloom et al. recommend: establishment of nursery schools to provide stimulus-rich environments as early as possible in life; specially designed curricula and specially trained teachers for this special type of nursery school and kindergarden; and parent involvement and education. Positing further recommendations to be instituted on the elementary school level, Bloom argues for early testing and diagnosis, varying approaches to introductory learning and special attention to the development of fundamental skills in language, reading, and arithmetic as well as developing general skills in learning itself.[25]

In the fifth section of *Compensatory Education for the Culturally Deprived*, the authors consider the special case of the Negro student. They believe that culturally deprived Negroes have an additional set of problems created by racial prejudice. Due to the vicious circle of racism, Negro students receive inadequate encouragement in the home and inferior or discriminatory treatment in the classroom. This results not only in a poor self-image but often in self-contempt. The cumulative effects of these socio-economic conditions are keenly evident in the classroom. One little girl in Kohl's *36 Children* could not understand why anyone would want to teach her or her classmates. Others in the same class expressed great fear of the process of education and disappointment over the relationship between the races.[26] Naturally, such tensions and doubts among culturally deprived Negroes would have immeasurably adverse effects on their education. As first steps in mitigating this situation, Bloom et al. argue for the integration of neighborhoods and schools, warm and supportive professional staffs, and adequate vocational training, guidance, and placement.

Adolescence brings additional problems to the culturally deprived. As a youngster grows out of childhood he becomes aware that he is a social entity distinct from his primary group. This realization leaves him with a need to crystallize his identity and to establish his own adequacy as a male or female in our society. In a system such as ours this adequacy is related to the ability to enter a vocation which will allow self-support and the taking of a wife. Occupational opportunities are limited for the culturally deprived adolescent and, according to Bloom, schools are not providing sufficient help to rectify the situation. To aid culturally deprived adolescents in the vocational arena, schools should: identify and tutor those culturally deprived students who can complete secondary education and begin higher education; allow for specialization in an area where an individual is particularly interested; and institute work-study programs with industry and public agencies.[27]

As noted earlier, Fantini and Weinstein expand their investigation of the culturally deprived to include the poor, the Spanish-speaking, the Indian, the migrant, and a certain proportion of the middle class. The etiology of this cultural deprivation is examined in a chapter of their book *The Hidden Curriculum.* Fantini and Weinstein realize the importance of the linguistic atmosphere of a home. In many low-income homes, language, or rather its inadequate development, often condemns a child to a limited perspective of the world in which he lives. Drawing heavily on the sociolinguistic theory of Basil Bernstein, Fantini and Weinstein investigate rather thoroughly the role language plays in socialization. Bernstein identifies two modes of speech which exist in any language:

elaborated and restricted. An elaborated linguistic code tends to be highly articulated in terms of vocabulary and syntax while a restricted code has limited syntactical variation and a limited vocabulary as well. The child exposed at an early age to an elaborated style of speech learns to associate a wide array of word symbols with their referents and begins to perceive a relatively wider array of objects within his environment. Since an elaborated code makes wide use of adjectives, the child's perception is not only widespread but more articulated.

By contrast, a restricted linguistic code is limited in its vocabulary and syntactical alternatives and tends to avoid descriptive modifiers. Generalities often suffice for specific verbs and nouns. "Stop it" is likely to suffice for "Put the vase down before you break it." Bernstein states that these two modes of speech tend to develop qualitatively different perceptual orientations to the environment. A child familiar with an elaborated linguistic code is better equipped to handle abstractions, to think inductively and deductively. The user of a restricted code is relatively more dependent on his immediate perceptual experiences. He has a limited ability to manipulate word-symbols and therefore has a limited capacity for abstract learning. [28] Classroom learning, which is usually of an abstract nature, would come easier for the one child than the other.

Whereas learning disability might be traced to a particular linguistic code, it can also be attributed to a different language and culture altogether. Many "slow learners" in big city schools are Spanish-speaking. Not only must they contend with the difficulties of learning their own language, but they must try to learn abstractions through a language which is largely foreign to them. The language difference is complicated by cultural differences. Some Puerto Rican children are taught to bow their heads when being spoken to by an elder. Many American teachers, however, prefer to have a child look them in the eye when speaking to him. The same language and cultural differences, as well as poverty, complicate the educational progress of the American Indian. The Indian child is generally socialized into a traditional, tribal pattern of behavior. His entry into school represents an entry into an entirely different culture. The possibility of an Indian child becoming a marginal man greatly increases as a result of schooling. If he moves toward the institutional orientation, he may be viewed as trying to be a white man; if he maintains a tribal orientation he limits his mobility in the larger American society.[29]

The rural migrant child, aside from suffering from poverty and related factors, must contend with a life which is constantly on the move. He is seldom able to establish any permanency and often has difficulty grasping the concepts of home and property. His erratic life prevents him from considering school as an entity related to him and his future. When he starts school he is often older than other students. When he quits he is probably younger. Due to the constant migration of his parents, no continuity in the educational process is provided him. He is a stranger to the continuous and developmental learning process of the schools. Although his peripatetic life may provide him with a rich variety of experiences, many of which potentially equal those provided in a formal curriculum, he probably benefits little educationally due to lack of adult guidance and interpretation. This problem of transiency also affects the urban poor who often move frequently within the city limits. Nevertheless, they remain in the same school system and generally find a certain degree of continuity from school to school. The migrant child, however, changes states and systems so often that there is little connectedness between the academic instruction he receives from year to year or month to month.

Fantini and Weinstein also consider the middle-class culturally deprived child. Although his material needs are well met in the comfort of suburban living, his experience can still be limited. The bland monotony of suburban living can limit a child's knowledge of the real world into which he will someday move. The lack of exposure to different cultures, values, and attitudes may prevent him from playing a productive and flexible role in adult life. Further evidence indicates an unrealistic orientation to money, career, and the intricacies of power and intergroup relations. Although the father is often present in the home, his excessive absence can offset the developmental role in the child's life he could have played. Finally, a child whose only contacts with diverse ethnic groups cast them in subordinate roles may have trouble adapting to a Negro who is not a laborer or a Chinaman who is not a launderer. The deprivation of the suburban youth is not as serious as that of the poor, Spanish-speaking, Indian, or migrant but, in some cases, the results can be just as damaging.[30]

Frank Riessman's book, *The Culturally Deprived Child*, served to awaken many educators to the problems of both teachers and students in urban ghetto schools. Riessman argues for a cultural approach to the education of the deprived child and suggests two major benefits. One has to do with the social-emotional relationship between the teacher and the child while the other is more directly concerned with the way subject matter can best be taught. A sound cultural understanding of the deprived student would enable the teacher to escape his middle-class biases and understand the actions of a child who is reacting in a more or less functional manner to the social environment in which he lives. Such an understanding of his culture would enable the teacher to plan a curriculum which, while relevant to the institution of education itself, would offer substantial interest and purpose to the culturally deprived child.[31] To explain and justify his contentions, Riessman guides his readers through an examination of the values, norms, and strong points of the cuturally deprived.

Riessman begins by attacking the popular belief that the culturally deprived child is not interested in education. Quoting his own and others' research, Riessman tells us that education is valued by the culturally deprived. Responses to questionnaires and interviews indicate that a large percentage of adults in lower socioeconomic homes are concerned that their children do well in school. [32] Establishing that education is valued, Riessman suggests we take a new look at the culture of the underprivileged. Rather than focusing on the negative aspects of their culture, he suggests we emphasize and appreciate other themes in the life of the culturally deprived. The underprivileged in our society are basically traditional and conservative. They have fixed notions about the role of women, punishment, custom, diet, and the world in general. Because of the inability of the culturally deprived adult to alter the course of things, he comes to believe that the world, rather than himself, is responsible for his misfortunes. Consequently, he is less apt to suffer pangs of self-blame and can be more direct in his expressions of aggression. His practical orientation toward life does not encourage abstract ideas. Due to his anti-intellectualism, he is much more physical and motoric in both his learning episodes and his communication with others. Closely related to this physical bias is the emphasis on masculinity and the use of physical force to settle disputes. The poverty of the underprivileged's life is extensive. Yet, this same poverty leads to certain positive factors in the socialization of the young.

In the home of the underprivileged, there are many children and there are many parent substitutes. The large extended family provides a small world in which one is accepted and safe. The atmosphere is highly communal and very cooperative. Sibling rivalry and fear of a new baby brother seems less intense than in middle-class homes. There also appears to be far less jealousy and competitiveness. Furthermore, Riessman argues, the physical nature of punishment does not make a child feel unloved because he has done something wrong. That is, he can be loved *and* be wrong. In homes where love is withdrawn as a punishment for wrongdoing, a child can become highly insecure.[33]

Riessman asserts that the culturally deprived child is more educable than is popularly believed. Essentially, he argues that a major problem of appreciating the potentialities of the underprivileged is the current use of biased I.Q. measures further complicated by little test "know-how" on the part of many students. In the area of testing, Riessman seems to think the following changes should be made: increased employment of performance tests; use of "culture fair" tests; revamping of deficiencies of standard

I.Q. tests; establishing rapport with the culturally deprived and developing in them test-taking habits; and, finally, placing less emphasis on standard I.Q.'s and attempting to discover the child's "hidden I.Q."[34]

Riessman also considers the case of the "slow gifted child." In contemporary school systems, the culturally deprived are often considered poor learners when, in fact, they are not poor but slow. The approach to such a student by many educators is quite ineffective. The emphasis on speed should be dropped. By rushing the slow learner and by categorizing him prematurely, the slow learner may become the poor learner. To avoid this result, school systems should make curricula changes to allow for extended learning processes. Riessman also believes the underprivileged individual is more verbal than usually assumed. Underprivileged children are quite good with descriptive adjectives, colorful slang, and spontaneous, unstructured expressions. In order to take advantage of their linguistic skills, the teacher should try to integrate their style with more formal English rather than replace it.

Riessman makes several suggestions related to teaching style in underprivileged areas. He believes a teacher should be consistent, straightforward, and clearly define what is to be done in class. At the same time he should be warm, informal, and down-to-earth. He must also realize his "value problem" and respect the beliefs and sentiments of students. One of his big tasks in "breaking through the cultural barrier" is gaining rapport and winning the support of natural classroom leaders. Once he has done this, however, he should remember that the underprivileged do not have an auditory set which inclines them to listen to lectures for minutes on end. He will have to teach them how to listen. He should also develop their verbal skills by taking advantage of their physical pattern of communication. The idea is to *build* on the abilities already possessed by the underprivileged. Teachers of the underprivileged should also attempt to dispel the intense fear of failure held by so many students. They should somehow identify with them and consider students as individuals rather than as mere recipients of information.[35]

Not only do the underprivileged come to school under adverse socio-economic conditions, their psychological set often disinclines them to the type of educational instruction available. A great deal of attention has been given to what educators call "need for achievement," commonly designated as "n Ach." Certainly, this need for achievement should be discussed with relation to school and schoolwork. Culturally deprived children may have strong desires to succeed in various social areas and, therefore, it cannot be said they have no "n Ach." The point is, however, that this need is often missing where school and schoolwork are concerned. The culturally deprived often maintain an intense loyalty to a group in which there may be discouragement of individual effort and initiative. School, which often represents an alien or hostile culture to the underprivileged, is not something for which group norms are to be sacrificed. If achieving means being successful in academic competition, such students prefer not to achieve.[36] The absence of "n Ach," in school settings can be traced to the anti-intellectualism often predominant in the homes of the culturally deprived. Although some lower-class parents and students maintain a defiant, hostile attitude toward school and school authorities, most of them make at least a show of compliance. They are, after all, members of a national culture in which school is considered necessary. They may not understand why school is valued, or what relevance it has to their life, but they understand enough to know that children should be sent to school and "behave themselves" while there. Indeed, parents of the culturally deprived are often more concerned that their children behave than do well academically. Whereas a middle-class mother might exhort her child to "get all your arithmetic problems correct today," a culturally deprived parent would say, "Behave and don't get into trouble."[37]

Another psychological set which profoundly affects the education of the culturally deprived is their preference for immediate rather than delayed gratification. Due to their relative inability to manipulate symbols and move about in the world of the abstract, rewards for learning episodes must be immediate and concrete. Commonly used delayed reinforcements such as grades, gold stars, or honor rolls do not reward the underprivileged child. For him to associate activity with a positive response, such response must be immediate. Due to the nature of their environment, culturally deprived children are required to appreciate and prefer concrete benefits as opposed to those which are delayed or abstract. In fact, this is the case with most members of their social class.[38] Such behavior not only develops from the requirements of their hand-to-mouth pattern of living, but also because their primary group socializes them in this manner.

A poor self-concept can also impair learning. Thomas describes the case of an eleven-year-old who was far behind his classmates in school work, retained infantile behavior his classmates had long since abandoned, and constituted a general behavior problem. The boy was subjected to extensive clinical analysis which revealed that although he had a normal intelligence, he had a poor self-concept and lacked even a moderate degree of confidence. An early physical problem had prevented him from grasping the fundamentals of reading. Subsequent school failure produced in the boy's mind a distorted picture of himself and of the best ways to react to his environment. In his desperation, he stumbled on infantilism as an adjustment mechanism. His behavior caused him greater failure in school which, in turn, led to increased infantilism. The boy was caught in a "vicious circle" from which he required help to escape. Diagnosticians decided the boy needed to replace his current low estimate of personal worth with a new self-concept. To accomplish this, three things were in order: He needed to be provided a way in which he could vent his frustrations without alienating others; he needed to be treated like a youth whose infantile tendencies would not be catered to; and he needed to be subjected to a highly concentrated remedial reading program.[39]

The underachieving boy was subjected to a four point program. First, he was started on tasks at which it was known he would succeed. As he eventually realized that he could perform adequately on certain levels, he was given more sophisticated and varied material. Second, he was not required to stay too long at one activity so that he would not become bored or frustrated. The teacher served as a supervisor, providing him and other pupils in the class with special and more extensive personal help. The boy was also encouraged to be self-reliant while infantile episodes were ignored or treated in a mildly disfavorable manner. Whenever he encountered a serious reading problem, he was encouraged to study it again. If and when he did come up with the solution, the instructor pointed out, "You did that yourself; I didn't do it. You did, and you did it well." The boy was also helped to face his shortcomings honestly and attempt to improve them. Parallel with the classroom experiences, he attended weekly sessions at a special clinic where he took part in personal interviews with a therapist and worked with other children in art and construction activities. At the end of a year, his reading ability had improved by at least two years.[40]

Closely related to this discussion of a poor self-concept is Goffman's research on the problems of identity suffered by many socially stigmatized individuals. By stigmatized, Goffman refers to those who possess attributes commonly termed disfavorable by the society at large. There are three grossly different types of stigmas. First, there are physical deformities. Next there are blemishes of individual character perceived as weak will, dishonesty, or treachery. Finally, there are the tribal stigma of race, nation, and religion. The stigmatized would generally include the physically deformed, the prostitute, the ex-mental-patient, the drug user, and, in some areas of this country, the Negro.[41] The central feature of the stigmatized individual's situation in life is a fear of "acceptance." In an educational setting, anxiety produced by one's belief that he is stigmatized can lead to learning disability. Depending on how he reacts to his insecure position, the stigmatized individual's behavior ranges from overly aggressive and boisterous to excessive timidity and withdrawal. Goffman believes that the stigmatized individual can be helped to make a "good adjustment" to his position in life. To do this, he must cheerfully and unselfconsciously accept himself as essentially the same as "normals." At the same time, he should voluntarily withhold himself from those situations in which others would find it difficult to give lip service to their similar acceptance of him.[42]

There are a variety of other psychological theories related to the etiology of learning disability. Many of them are highly abstract, however, and rather Freudian in nature. Some theorists propose that a disability to learn is the result of Oedipal difficulties or characterizes an anal-retentive personality. Others believe learning disability is the result of extreme neurosis and other functional disorders. More widely accepted, however, are theories relating to the institution of education itself. Rather than placing the responsibility for learning disability on the pupil himself, the fault is seen to lie with the system and its methods.

3. Institutional

In most cases of learning disability, a failure to read properly is involved. If one is unable to read, he remains a stranger to the academic content of his books and to most classroom proceedings. Terman and Walcutt believe that the reading problem is the key to learning disability and furthermore, that reading problems can be traced to one single cause. It is purely a question of teaching method. To argue their case, Terman and Walcutt describe the method by which reading is currently taught. They then analyze problems related to this method and suggest a new instructional procedure.

Children are taught to recognize the whole word as a visual and meaningful unit. Little attention is paid to the phonics of a word, (the letter combinations related to its pronunciation). The reading process is seen as a gradual development of the child's ability to make finer and finer visual discriminations. He is introduced to a series of vocabulary words, asked to use them in a meaningful context and then to associate the spoken word with its written counterpart. Through practice and drill, the child establishes the habit of looking for and reacting to small visual differences between words. He learns to distinguish "bell" from "ball" because the sense of words can be changed by "a's" and "e's." Essentially, the process of learning to read is a process of associating the whole, written word with the proper pronunciation and meaning. Little attention is paid to the letter configurations except when they are used as visual clues to differentiate various words.[43]

This method of reading instruction finds its theoretical justification in Gestalt psychology, which is supposed to demonstrate that the child learns from wholes to parts. A child first discriminates an object or a person as a whole. Later, he learns to discriminate between different parts of different wholes, thus allowing him to tell one whole from another. According to the Gestalt-based system, it is improper to teach the letters first because to do so would reverse the fundamental learning process. The child trained to look for letters instead of whole words would have his attention captured by these small objects and fail to look at the whole words out of which meaning is made.

According to Terman and Walcutt, Gestalt psychology is misapplied where learning to read is concerned. A child taught to read by the discrimination of visual clues has memorized words by looking at the shapes of various letters or, in some cases, by the spaces between some letters. The desired transition from seeing a word as a total pattern to seeing it as a sequence of letters often confuses and bewilders him. For the child who does not know the alphabet either as printed letters or symbols of sounds, an unfamiliar word is a totally new "squiggle" presented to him as a meaning and, therefore, as a completely new learning act unrelated to anything else he knows. The whole process of learning new words seems to him extraordinarily arbitrary since he has no way of knowing why one squiggle means cow and another boat. The vital link of sound has been omitted. This is because the sound of a word is in the letters and the current application of Gestalt psychology forbids beginning with anything so small as a letter.[44]

Terman and Walcutt suggest that the child be taught, step by step, a complete system of phonics. Rather than emphasizing linguistic rules, he should be made familiar with all the phonograms (as, at, ite, ine, etc.). The next step is to show him that he can read one-syllable words at sight without having to "sound them out." This system would result, not in analyzing or breaking up into syllables, but in instant recognition. The basic process is to form an association between the sounds of the spoken word and the letters representing the sounds and then to connect these two with the meaning. It is the meaning which makes the word a whole, and one which can be remembered more easily. Instruction should begin by teaching the child the names and appearances of the letters of the alphabet. Once he is familiar with them, he should be taught compound phonetic symbols and their appropriate pronunciation. He should learn that "c" says "cuh" and "a" says "a" and "t" says "tuh." Looking at the word "cat," he can hardly help from arriving at the proper pronunciation. He must also be taught to see "pl" as a unit and that the two letters "ay" have a single sound. Thus, the word "play" would be more quickly recognized and pronounced. A good way to gauge the child's progress would be by having him read nonsense syllables.

It is also important to allow the child to develop at his own pace. He should not be allowed to flounder during his early learning experiences, but help should be supportive rather than directive. Terman and Walcutt further suggest that the teacher not overdo instruction in phonetics to the point where the word as a whole would not be pronounced properly. The child must learn to combine phonetic sounds into the smoothly-flowing pronunciation of a word.[45]

Other critics of the educational institution argue that students are often given certain types of instruction before their cognitive processes have been adequately developed. They maintain that a child should be introduced to new material only at given points in his intellectual development. For theoretical justification or their observations, the monumental research of Piaget is often quoted. Piaget sees four major steps in the growth of the human intellect.

From 0 to 2 years of age, the child passes through

the sensori-motor stage of development, which is divided into six phases. Eventually he begins to use foresight and symbolic representation. The second period of development is the preoperational stage (2 to 7 years), where the early forms of social behavior appear. Here, the child also begins to extract concepts from experiences and begins elementary intuitive thought. From age 7-8 to 11-12, the child passes through the operational stage of logical thinking. He begins to see relationships between the parts and the whole and can think in a highly abstract fashion. Finally, the child enters the stage of formal operations, which · is characterized by use of propositional and combinational operations. It is believed by many that these stages are related to the age and physical development of the child. Although each individual may grow at a different rate, his cognitive evolution generally includes the aforementioned stages in their proper order.[46]

Piaget himself believes that instruction must be designed to fit the individual's stage of development since the cognitive structure determines the degree of understanding that the child can bring to the solution of problems.[47]

Other educators have argued that learning disability is often the result of improper teaching procedures. They believe that Johann Herbart's theory of learning by association should be adhered to. Herbart's theory proposes five steps in the teaching process: (1) preparation, in which old ideas related to new material are called to the learner's mind; (2) presentation, the actual giving of new information; (3) association, in which new material is compared with and related to the old; (4) generalization, in which definitions or general principles are drawn from specifics; and (5) application, in which general principles are given meaning by reference to examples and practical situations.[48] Herbart's theory, however, has been severely criticized by many educators, notably John Dewey, who believed his procedures led to a failure to take natural growth and individual differences into account. Herbartian emphasis on method supposedly led to a "lock-step" school which so ordered the learning process that creativity was stifled.

Many educational psychologists and teachers have claimed that children are often wrongly classified as poor learners on the basis of their performance on I.Q. and other tests. There seems to be general confusion about what "intelligence" is, how it can best be measured and, indeed, whether it can be accurately measured at all. Further criticism of testing relates to the claim that tests constructed by middle-class educators cannot adequately measure abilities of lower-class children. Such tests are "culture-bound" and should not be used as a basis of classification. The great danger lies in the fact that some students are liable to be separated from their classmates and put on a slower track when, in fact, this is inappropriate.[49]

John Holt believes that failure in school is largely due to the curricula and attitudes which children face in an educational setting. Current educational practices foster bad strategies, raise children's fears, produce learning which is usually fragmented and distorted, and generally fail to meet the real needs of children.[50] Holt states that most children in school fail. Close to forty percent of those beginning high school drop out before graduation. One in three quit college. Except for a handful, who may or may not be good students, most develop only a small fraction of the tremendous capacity for learning, understanding, and creating with which they were born. Most children fail because they are afraid, bored, and confused. They are afraid, above all else, of failing and displeasing the anxious adults whose expectations hang over their heads in an oppressive fashion. They are bored because the things they do in school are dull, trivial, and unrelated to their needs. These children are confused because they are told many contradictory things during the course of an academic year and are constantly subjected to hypocrisy.

By requiring children to work for such contemptible rewards as gold stars or A's on report cards, educators encourage them to feel that the end and aim of all they do in school is nothing more than to get a good mark. By holding them to conventional educational processes, we kill their curiosity and their feeling that it is a good and admirable thing to be curious. Schools tend to be dishonest. Adults are often not honest with children, least of all in school. Even in the least controversial areas, textbooks give children a dishonest and distorted picture of the world. In response to this educational approach, children learn not to give what they believe are right answers, but the answers they think the teacher likes to hear. Holt also believes that teachers are dishonest about their own fears, prejudices, and limitations. This dishonesty affects the children and they, in turn, are also afraid to be honest. Controversial subjects, no matter how relevant to students' lives, are ignored and shunted aside.

According to Holt, schools should be a place where children learn what they most want to know instead of what teachers think they ought to know. There should be no set curriculum since most of what we teach in school is disregarded by students. Their failure to retain information (notwithstanding the fact that it is usually irrelevant) is due to the fact that there is no way to coerce children without making them afraid. If they are afraid they cannot learn in a healthy, constructive manner. Schools should be places where each child, in his own way, can satisfy his curiosity, develop his abilities and talents, pursue his interests, and get a glimpse of reality by interacting with other children and teachers as well. In short, schools must present a great smorgasbord of intellectual, artistic, creative, and athletic activities from which a child can take whatever and how much he wants.[51]

William Glasser closely examines the effect of failure in school on personal adjustment. If a child comes to be labeled, or labels himself, as a failure in school, he will be little motivated towards accomplishing other socially respected goals. He will not succeed in general until he can in some way first experience success in one important part of his life. Glasser believes that if any child, no matter what his background, can succeed in school, he has an excellent chance for success in life. If he fails at any stage of his education—elementary, junior and high school, or college—his chances for success in life are greatly diminished.[52] Accordingly, it is important that society provide schools where children, through a reasonable use of their capacities, can succeed. If this is not done, educators shall do little to solve the major problems of this country. At present, there are many factors inherent in our educational system which not only accelerate failure in school but cause it. This situation must be remedied by working within the current educational system, not by separating problem cases from the system and treating them independently.

Through the process of reality therapy, children should be helped to develop the capacity to love. They must also develop a feeling of self-worth. Traditional approaches to the problem child will not work. Reality therapy helps the student examine his own behavior in a real manner and decide whether such behavior is helping anything or anybody. When he makes a value judgment on this matter and commits himself to change, no excuse is acceptable for not following through. Neither school nor therapist should manipulate the world so that the child does not suffer the reasonable consequences of his behavior.

In order to help children succeed in school, educational material should be relevant to their lives. It should be capable of motivating them. They should also be helped to understand that what they learn in life can also be relevant to school. In short, they must see school and life as a highly intertwined process of learning. Today, grades are so important that they, rather than learning, are often sought after. Glasser suggests a superior-pass system in which nobody can fail. Inadequate performance is not recorded by the school. The student merely repeats the course until such time as he passes or performs in a superior fashion. In this way no student is ever labeled a failure, and his confidence is less exposed to serious damage. Furthermore, material in class should be covered in more depth, even though this means reducing the total amount of material in the curriculum. This would serve to emphasize the ability to think rather than the ability to memorize. Whenever possible, students with behavior problems should be treated in heterogeneous groups rather than singled out for special treatment (and thus being identified as failures). In terms of reading disability, however, homogenous groups may be more appropriate.

Finally, Glasser suggests that teachers regularly lead students in nonjudgmental classroom discussions about what is important and relevant to them. There are three types of classroom meetings: social-problem-solving, concerned with school behavior; open-ended, concerned with intellectually important subjects; and educational-diagnostic, where concepts of curriculum can be discussed.[53]

Other criticisms not necessarily restricted to teaching methods have been directed at the institution of education. Patricia Sexton believes educational administrators have not been duly concerned with equal education for both the rich and poor. Essentially, she states that the education and treatment a child receives is directly related to his social class standing. Drawing from her research in a large midwestern city, she writes that more money is spent by school boards for schools located in upper-income areas than for those in poorer neighborhoods. In low-income high schools students often drop out before graduation. This is not the case in upper-income areas where students stay to graduation and receive more services. Sexton also claims that buildings and facilities in upper-class areas are superior to those in depressed neighborhoods. Club activities, "gifted child" programs, evening and summer school programs, and various other educational services seem to be more extensive in higher-income schools. More money is spent on teachers' salaries in these schools, since inexperienced substitute teachers, who are heavily concentrated in low-income areas, receive less in wages and fringe benefits.[54]

As a first step in providing equal educational opportunity to all children, Sexton proposes that school expenditures be equalized, at the very least, among the various income groups. She then makes thirty-seven other suggestions for improving and equalizing education. These include: hiring teachers and administrators with zeal for helping lower-income students; abandoning use of I.Q. tests; reduction of class size and elimination of most segregated groupings and curricula; free books and medical care for those in need; expansion of experiential opportunities and involvement on a personal level with parents and students.[55]

James Conant, former president of Harvard University, reports a tremendous disparity in educational services between the slum and the suburb. His major tenet is that the status and ambitions of parents determine to a considerable extent what a school should and can do.[56] Due to the economic position and level of aspiration of the upper-income classes, their children recieve greater opportunities to advance educationally than do the children of lower-income families. Nevertheless, Conant believes that suburban students have educational problems which are in need of remedy. He feels that the main problem in wealthy suburban schools is to guide the parent whose college ambitions outrun his child's abilities toward a realistic idea of what kind of education his child is suited for. An expansion of the California pattern of higher education, which includes two-year junior colleges and sophisticated vocational training, would help to solve many problems. With regard to conditions in the slums, Conant states that we are allowing "social dynamite" to accrue. More money should be given to slum schools and they should be made responsible for educational and vocational guidance of youth after they leave school until age twenty-one. More attention ought to be paid to developing meaningful courses for pupils with less than average abilities. Should these students acquire salable skills, the federal government must allocate funds to open employment opportunities on a nondiscriminatory basis. The decentralization of school administration in big cities, as well as the establishment of nonpolitical and high-minded school boards, should round out these efforts.[57]

C. AN ANALYSIS OF COMPENSATORY EDUCATION

Compensatory education programs are quite widespread in American school systems. Although there are many and varied approaches and methodologies, the format for most programs seems to have been set by the Higher Horizons project originally sponsored by the city of New York in 1956. The intent of Higher Horizons (initially called The Demonstration Guidance Projects) was to identify able students from lower-income families and guide them toward college. The project was soon expanded to include all levels of schools. Essentially, Higher Horizons was designed to broaden the perspectives of its participants and instill in them a more favorable attitude towards education. A number of somewhat novel approaches were employed. Nonverbal I.Q. tests were used to assess the abilities of students. In order to instill motivation and improve the children's self-image, pictures of eminent Negroes and Puerto Ricans were displayed in the classrooms. Reading deficits were treated by holding special reading classes with a teacher-student ratio of 1:5. An intensive counseling service was provided to inform students of college and career opportunities. To broaden perspectives, book fairs and circulating libraries were started in the schools. The students were also subjected to an intensive cultural program which not only exposed them to the practice but the theory of music and art. In order to give children an opportunity for quiet study, classrooms were opened after school hours.

Higher Horizons also provided for daytime meetings of teachers and parents. In order to gain their cooperation, parents were fully informed of the purpose of the project. If parents could not attend the daytime meetings they were visited at home by social caseworker or counselor. Newsletters and workshops were formed to keep parents up-to-date. Where family conditions did not favor studying, counselors worked out agreements to turn off television sets during certain hours and persuaded younger family members to permit students to work without interruption.[58]

There is a basic similarity between all compensatory education programs, from those aimed at preschool children to those dealing with college students. There are a number of modifications made within each program, however, depending on the ages and experiential backgrounds of the subjects. The Infant Education Research Project carried on in Washington, D. C., tutored children ranging in age from fifteen to thirty-six months. In coordination with an educational supervisor, each child was instructed on a one-to-one basis, one hour a day, five days a week. The tutor talked with the child, showed him pictures, taught new words, played games, read from books, assisted in coloring pictures and putting together simple jigsaw puzzles, and the like. Mothers and other members of the child's family were encouraged to participate.[59] Project Headstart programs, which deal primarily with preschool children from three to five years old, expose their subjects to a series of new and varied experiences. This experience enrichment is coupled with a program of tutoring aimed at preparing the underprivileged child for the school atmosphere.

On the elementary school level, the Augmented Reading Project in Pomona, California, focused on raising the reading scores of children in grades one through three. Because of the special problems involved in teaching disadvantaged children, major emphasis was placed on teacher in-service training. This included six meetings to acquaint teachers with the community and its ethnic groups, summer workshops devoted to the history and culture of ethnic groups, institutes for remedial reading teachers, in-service training for aides, and a series of discussions for administrators. The teachers were also advised by a panel of Negro parents and a consultant from the University of Southern California.[60]

Many secondary school compensatory education projects are designed to prepare disadvantaged students for postsecondary education. The Summer Upward Bound Project in Terre Haute, Indiana, moved seventy-five high school students into dormitories at Indiana State University for eight weeks. The first summer involved a highly structured curriculum with lessons in language arts, mathematics, study methods and techniques, and perceptual skills. Time was also allotted for extracurricular activities such as play rehearsals and concerts. Students enrolled in Summer Upward Bound for three consecutive summers. There were also followup programs during the regular school year.[61]

Various forms of compensatory education continue on college levels. Many institutions of higher education operate programs designed to help the underprivileged student matriculate. Academic requirements are often lowered to allow selected individuals initial entry to college study. Through a series of diagnostic tests and appropriate tutelage, an attempt is made to compensate for the student's often limited academic background. Certain graduate and professional schools sponsor introductory summer programs aimed at putting disadvantaged applicants on a more equal footing with those from higher socioeconomic classes.

Although compensatory education is a mammoth and constantly growing enterprise, it has been criticized from many quarters. A report by the Washington Research Project of the Southern Center for Studies in Public Policy and the NAACP Legal Defense and Educational Fund, Inc., found that compensatory education programs funded by ESEA fail to benefit the underprivileged child. The report claims that money earmarked for compensatory education is being diverted to pay for normal operating costs of many school districts. Furthermore, according to this report, thousands of dollars of Title I money are allocated to affluent schools where not a single educationally disadvantaged child is enrolled.[62] The Commission on Civil Rights reported in 1967 that compensatory education programs have not been effective. The commission cited as causes of this failure the fact that many programs fail to attack the racial and social isolation in schools which, in fact, gives rise to the educationally disadvantaged.[63]

Others have criticized compensatory education not only on the basis of its administration but because it often fails to produce tangible and durable improvement. Wolf and Wolf have written that too much is expected of compensatory programs and that there is a tendency to exaggerate the nature and scope of the influence schools can actually wield in the improvement of educational

alternatives.[64]   Fantini and Weinstein report that people
who are responsible for compensatory education projects
often reveal that progress is less than satisfactory. These
authors liken the disadvantaged child to a poorly
constructed automobile. Just as an automotive rehabilitation division would not solve the problem for a
manufacturer, compensatory education cannot solve the
problem for society. If something is not properly prepared
to function originally, it never will function according to
par.[65]

After conducting an extensive survey of compensatory
education programs across the country, Edmund Gorden
wrote ". . . despite all our current efforts, tremendous gains
are not being achieved. We are probably failing because we
have not yet found the right answers." He goes on to state
that many evaluations of compensatory programs are
based more on sentiment than fact.[66]   In a pointed survey
of opinions and programs, Roger Freeman states that
compensatory education is an unqualified failure. He
reports that where gains in verbal areas have appeared,
they disappear within a few months. To support this
statement, he refers to studies by Dr. Gerald Alpern,
director of Research Child Psychiatry Services at Indiana
University Medical School, and Dr. Max Wolf of the New
York Center for Urban Education. These studies, however,
were limited to children participating in selected Headstart
programs.[67]

The U. S. Office of Education does little to clear up the
controversy over the efficacy of compensatory education.
Although Congress ordered annual evaluations of ESEA,
Title I, in 1967, the reports have often been vague or
innocuous. A recent report stated, "It is still impossible,
for example, to reach fully valid conclusions about the
national impact upon participating pupils from programs
provided with Title I funds. Nationally representative
information about pupil benefits derived from these
programs simply does not exist."[68]   The reactions of
certain government officials have been much more pointed
and critical. At the beginning of 1970, the President of the
United States made a report to Congress on the nation's

compensatory education programs. Essentially, Mr. Nixon rated compensatory education as a total failure and suggested that more research should be conducted before continuing expenditures.[69]

Perhaps the best way to illustrate the nature of the controversy over compensatory education is to follow the history of a single program. The More Effective Schools program (MES) in New York City began as the brainchild of the United Federation of Teachers and the American Federation of Teachers. The plans for the program were offered in March, 1963, to the New York City Board of Education as a counterproposal to the board's offer of $1,000 "combat pay" to lure 2,000 experienced teachers into slum schools to fill vacancies. In the spring of 1964, the UFT met and submitted a plan for MES. The report of the committee "was in response to community agitation and expression of discontent with schools in ghetto areas in New York City."[70] The major objective of MES was to increase the academic achievement of pupils by means of modern teaching methods under optimum conditions with a staff of enthusiastic teachers and clinical teams and to instill "in the pupils a desire for learning, a liking for school and increased respect for themselves and others."[71]

There have been several evaluations of the More Effective Schools program since its inception. The United Federation of Teachers and the American Federation of Teachers have consistently upheld the program. In 1965, the Board of Education conducted an investigation which indicated that children were making greater gains than ever before. A 1966-1967 evaluation by David Fox, however, reported that the MES program had no significant effect on pupil learning or performance.[72] This view was expressed in an earlier report by Gloria Channen, an MES teacher. She boldly criticized all aspects of the program, from test results to difficulty of ordering supplies to lack of teacher training and orientation.[73] In January of 1969 Roger Freeman also commented that MES was ineffective.[74] A more recent evaluation of MES, which appeared in the September, 1970, issue of *American*

Teacher, contradicted Freeman by reporting that enthusiasm for learning had been aroused.[75]

Within the next few years, there will probably be a continuance of contradictory reports on the efficacy of More Effective Schools. Whether or not that particular program is indeed successful remains hard to determine at this point. A question of equal importance, however, involves our basic inability to arrive at a consensus. Why is it that scores of qualified and professional educators remain in disagreement with one another regarding either MES in particular or compensatory education in general? Possible answers to this question will be explored in a subsequent chapter.

FOOTNOTES

1. Robert Havighurst, "Who are the Socially Disadvantaged?" in *The Disadvantaged Child: Issues and Innovations*, ed. by Joe L. Frost and Glenn R. Hawkes (Boston: Houghton Mifflin Company, 1966), pp. 20-21.
2. Willard Abraham, *The Slow Learner* (New York: The Center for Applied Research in Education, 1964), p. 18.
3. *ibid*, pp. 4-5.
4. Mario D. Fantini and Gerald Weinstein, *The Disadvantaged: Challenge to Education* (New York: Harper and Row Publishers, Inc., 1968), p. 10.
5. "18 Million Have Reading Woes," *Daily Tribune* (Royal Oak, Michigan), Saturday, September 12, 1970, p. 1.
6. Frank Riessman, *The Culturally Deprived Child* (New York: Harper and Row, Publishers, Inc., 1962), p. 1.
7. Fantini and Weinstein, *op. cit.*, p. 12.
8. Abraham, *op. cit.*, p. 3.
9. Havighurst, *op. cit.*, p. 21.
10. Edmund W. Gordon and Doxey A. Wilkerson, *Compensatory Education for the Disadvantaged* (New York: College Entrance Examination Board, 1966), pp. 4-5.
11. *ibid.*, p. 8.
12. For a more extensive review of the national development of these programs, see L. D. Crow, W. I. Murray, and H. H. Smythe, eds., *Educating the Culturally Disadvantaged Child* (New York: David McKay, 1966), pp. 148-202.
13. "Headstart for Children in the Slums," *American Education*, I (December, 1964/January, 1965), pp. 30-31.
14. "The First Work of These Times," *American Education*, I (April, 1965), p. 14.
15. Joy Connors, "They're On Their Way," *American Education*, VI (June, 1970), p. 24.
16. Estimate of Dr. Edward T. Sigler, Director of the Office of Child

Development for U. S. Department of Health, Education and Welfare.

17. Gordon and Wilkerson, *op. cit.*, p. 157.

18. Ernest R. Hilgard, *Introduction to Psychology* (3rd ed.; New York: Harcourt, Brace & World, Inc., 1962), p. 423.

19. Roger Brown, *Social Psychology* (New York: The Free Press, 1965), pp. 187-189. Most psychologists believe I.Q. can be raised ten to fifteen points if a subject is provided with proper instruction and experience.

20. Arthur R. Jensen, "How Much Can We Boost I.Q. and Scholastic Improvement," *Harvard Educational Review*, XXXIX (Winter, 1969), pp. 1-123.

21. Eleanor P. Wolf and Leo Wolf, "Sociological Perspective on the Education of Culturally Deprived Children," in *The Disadvantaged Child: Issues and Innovations*, ed. by Joe L. Frost and Glenn R. Hawkes (Boston: Houghton Mifflin Company, 1966), p. 72.

22. Benjamin Bloom, Allison Davis, and Robert Hess, *Compensatory Education for Cultural Deprivation* (New York: Holt, Rinehart and Winston, Inc., 1965), pp. 4-5.

23. *ibid.*, pp. 10-11.

24. *ibid.*, pp. 12-16.

25. *ibid.*, pp. 17-28.

26. Herbert Kohl, *36 Children* (New York: The New American Library, 1967), pp. 3-28.

27. Bloom et al., *op. cit.*, pp. 36-40.

28. Fantini and Weinstein, *op. cit.*, pp. 49-51.

29. *ibid.*, pp. 67 and 78.

30. *ibid.*, pp. 68-71.

31. Riessman, *op. cit.*, pp. 7-8.

32. *ibid.*, pp. 10-ll.

33. *ibid.*, pp. 26-29, 36-41.

34. *ibid.*, pp. 60-62.

35. *ibid.*, pp. 81-88.

36. Henry C. Lindgren, *Educational Psychology in the Classroom* (3rd ed.; New York: John Wiley & Sons, Inc., 1967), p. 554.

37. *loc. cit.*.

38. Joseph Kahl, *The American Class Structure* (New York: Holt, Rhinehart and Winston, 1965), pp. 205-214.

39. R. Murray Thomas, *Aiding the Maladjusted Pupil* (New York: David McKay Company, Inc., 1967), pp. 113-115.

40. *ibid.*, p. 120.

41. Erving Goffman, *Stigma* (New Jersey: Prentice-Hall, Inc., 1963), pp. 3-5.

42. *ibid.*, p. 121.

43. Sibyl Terman and Charles C. Walcutt, *Reading: Chaos and Cure* (New York: McGraw-Hill Book Company, Inc., 1958), pp. 40-41.

44. *ibid.*, pp. 54-56.

45. *ibid.*, pp. 155-161.

46. Rolf Muus, *Theories of Adolescence* (2nd ed.; New York: Random House, 1968), pp. 154-161.

47. *ibid.*, p. 172.

48. Henry P. Smith, *Psychology in Teaching* (Englewood Cliffs: Prentice-Hall, Inc., 1954), pp. 259-263.
49. For an excellent investigation of ability testing, see Lee J. Cronbach, *Essentials of Psychological Testing* (3rd ed.; New York: Harper & Row, 1970), Chapters 7-9.
50. John Holt, *How Children Fail* (New York: Dell Publishing Co., Inc., 1964), p. 17.
51. *ibid.*, p. 222.
52. William Glasser, *Schools Without Failure* (New York: Harper & Row, Publishers, 1969), p. 5.
53. *ibid*, p. 122.
54. Patricia C. Sexton, *Education and Income* (New York: The Viking Press, 1960), pp. 253-254.
55. *ibid.*, pp. 267-275.
56. James B. Conant, *Slums and Suburbs* (New York: McGraw-Hill Book Company, 1961), p. 1.
57. *ibid.*, pp. 144-147.
58. Riessman, *op. cit.*, pp. 98-102.
59. U. S. Department of Health, Education and Welfare, *Summaries of Selected Compensatory Education Projects* (Washington, D. C.: U. S. Government Printing Office, 1970), p. 3.
60. *ibid.*, p. 23.
61. *ibid.*, p. 33.
62. Washington Research Project and NAACP Legal Defense and Educational Fund, Inc., *Title I of ESEA: Is It Helping Poor Children* (2nd ed.; Washington, 1969), p. 58.
63. Quoted by F. M. Hechinger in "Integrated vs. Compensated," *New York Times*, February 26, 1967, p. E9.
64. Wolf and Wolf, *op. cit.*, p. 67.
65. Fantini and Weinstein, *op. cit.*, pp. 225-227.
66. Edmund W. Gordon, "Is Compensatory Education Failing?" *College Board Review*, LXII (Winter, 1966-67), p. 7.
67. Roger A. Freeman, "Dead End in American Education," *National Review*, XXI (January 14, 1969), p. 23.
68. U. S. Department of Health, Education and Welfare, *Education of the Disadvantaged: An Evaluative Report on Title I Elementary and Secondary Education Act of 1965* (Washington, D. C.: U. S. Government Printing Office, 1970), p. 6.
69. As reported by John Neary, "A Scientist's Variations on a Disturbing Racial Theme," *Life*, June 12, 1970, p. 58D.
70. David J. Fox, "Evaluating the More Effective Schools," *Phi Delta Kappa*, IL (June, 1968), p. 593.
71. "MES: A New Vote of Confidence," *American Teacher*, LV (September, 1970), p. 14.
72. "Controversy Over the More Effective Schools: A Special Supplement," *The Urban Review*, II (May, 1968), p. 17.
73. Gloria Channen, "The More Effective Schools," *The Urban Review*, II (February, 1967), pp. 23-26.
74. Freeman, *op. cit.*, p. 23.
75. *American Teacher*, September, 1970, *op. cit.*, p. 14.

V. RESOCIALIZATION IN CRIMINOLEGAL SYSTEMS: CRIMINAL REHABILITATION

A. NATURE AND EXTENT OF THE PROBLEM

1. The Recidivist

Resocialization in the criminolegal systems is generally referred to as rehabilitation. When an individual is defined as "criminal," the criminolegal systems are called upon to intervene and adjust his behavior until it conforms to a socially acceptable pattern. If this process of rehabilitation is successful, the individual will never again be adjudged guilty of a crime. If he commits a subsequent violation, he is considered to be a recidivist. The recidivist is considered to be the true problem for the criminolegal systems since, ipso facto, initial attempts at resocializing him have failed. The mere existence of recidivism implies that the criminolegal systems are not effective in their programs of behavior intervention and thus presents a threat to the institution.

Recidivists tend to exhibit a number of common characteristics. The younger the subject at the time of first conviction, the greater his chances are of repeating. Of the offenders under twenty released from the federal system in 1963, seventy-four percent were rearrested by 1969, as were seventy-two percent of those twenty to twenty-four years of age and sixty-nine percent of the offenders twenty-five to twenty-nine years.[1] In terms of race, the Negro rearrest rate was seventy-one percent while the Caucasian rate was sixty-one percent. All other races (primarily Indian Americans) had a rearrest rate of eighty-two percent.[2] Of the 1,419 female offenders released in 1963, forty-seven percent had been rearrested for new offenses by 1969. Other social, economic, and historical backgrounds seem to characterize the recidivist. The earlier an offender of any age leaves home, the more likely he is to continue in crime, all else being equal. The older a man is when released from prison, the less likely he is to return to crime. Marital status is also related to recidivism. The married individual living with his spouse is a better statistical risk than one who is single, separated, divorced, or widowed.[3] Employment habits prior to conviction and type of offense committed also have a relationship to recidivism. Those with substantial work experience are less likely to offend again. The most recidivistic crime category consists of crime against property (economic offenses) not involving violence. The more recidivistic an individual has been, the greater the chance that he will recidivate. Thus the offender with a long record of arrests and convictions is a less favorable risk than first offenders. Finally, studies suggest that the higher the socioeconomic status of a probationer's or parolee's family, the more likely he is to succeed under supervision.[4] Since less than half of actual crimes are reported, and less than twenty percent of those reported are solved, it is difficult even to estimate the number of criminal recidivists in the American population.[5] With respect to the known criminal population, however, studies of the yearly intake of prisons, reformatories, and jails show that from one-half to two-thirds of those imprisoned have served previous sentences.[6] In one major city, one-third of the persons arraigned on felony warrants were either on probation, parole, or out on bond awaiting court action in another case. Half of the inmates in the municipal jail had more than one warrant pending against them.[7]

The costs of crime are staggering. Crimes against property and business (excluding white-collar and organized crime) were responsible for economic losses of 13.1 billion dollars in 1969. Considering the fact that these types of crimes are most likely to be committed by the recidivist, one can understand why criminal rehabilitation has become such a critical social need.[8] Most police officials consider the recidivist to be the number one crime problem. Of the 5 billion dollars spent annually in the operation of police forces across the nation, at least half is related to the apprehension of the recidivist.[9]

The Federal Government has taken note of the increasing crime problem and expressed its concern by the passage of the Omnibus Crime Control and Safe Streets Act of 1968. Through this act, the Federal Government intends to grant 236 million dollars in aid to state and local law enforcement and criminal rehabilitation agencies. The government estimates it will spend 426 million dollars by 1971.[10] Concern with criminal rehabilitation is not a recent innovation. For hundreds of years now, Anglo-American criminolegal systems have been making concerted and varied attempts to achieve some form of resocialization.

2. History and Scope of Criminal Rehabilitation

Criminal rehabilitation can take place either in the subject's natural habitat or in some institutional or other artificial setting. The degree of rehabilitation which takes place in a prison environment is not encouraging and for that reason, more and more judges are considering probation as their first sentence alternative. The same belief is becoming widespread among prison officials and, whenever possible, they will consider a subject's early release on parole. Probation and parole are generally considered to be the optimum plan in criminal rehabilitation. If a judge chooses not to incarcerate an individual on the premise that he will not repeat a crime, the offender is placed on probation. If a corrections commission decides that a subject has served a sufficient amount of time in prison, he is released on parole. Both imply supervision of a subject's social adjustment, with threat of incarceration if a minimal amount of rehabilitation is not forthcoming. The major difference between probation and parole is that the former is prior to incarceration while the latter is after it.

The notion of probation has a history which dates back to early English common law. Certain historical judicial expedients may be mentioned as precursors of probation. The so-called "benefit of clergy" was a special plea whereby offenders of certain categories could claim exemption from, or mitigation of, punishment by a secular authority. The "judicial reprieve" was a temporary suspension by the court of either the imposition or execution of a sentence. Although it provided for only a temporary stay of imposition, it occasionally led to abandonment of prosecution. "Recognizance" is an old English legal device which obligated a subject to give assurance of a financial nature that, if released, he would not offend again. If there were a recurrence of crime, the subject would be indebted to the state for the designated amount and might also be incarcerated.[11] Other devices were "bail," the releasing of a prisoner in someone's custody in order to ensure appearance in court, and "filing of cases," which was a practice of suspending sentences peculiar to Massachusetts. These judicial precedents became popular in the United States, where, in 1841, John Augustus took a drunkard out on bail with promises to the court that the man's condition would improve. It did and the court of Boston took notice. By 1878, the first probation law was passed. By 1900, five states had legally recognized probation. By 1950, 43 states of the union made regular use of probation departments.[12] Today all 50 states and the Commonwealth of Puerto Rico administer probation departments.

The practice of parole did not develop from any specific source or experiment but from a number of independent judicial measures. Early in the 17th century, English courts began pardoning felons to help fulfill the demands for labor in the colonies of the New World. These newly pardoned individuals generally became indentured servants upon their arrival in America. After the Revolutionary War the British began transporting men to Australia for work on government projects and, later, to work for free settlers. In the latter 18th and early 19th century, "tickets-of-leave" came into widespread use. The first "ticket-of-leave" was merely a declaration signed by the governor dispensing a convict from government work and enabling him, on condition of supporting himself, to seek employment in a specified district. Eventually, the release of these felons was accompanied by supervision of their daily behavior. These legal activities had not gone unnoticed in the United States, which was itself considering some form of early and conditional release for selected inmates. By 1876, officials of the Elmira Reformatory in New York were designing a penal system based on the "indeterminate sentence." Although encountering a certain degree of opposition, the practice of early release coupled with supervision became firmly established in that state and eventually spread across the country. By 1900, twenty-six states had adopted these measures.[13] Today, all 50 states and the Commonwealth of Puerto Rico release prisoners on parole.

Probation and parole did not gain easy acceptance either in England or the United States. Nevertheless, popular opinion eventually began to support these practices and, as a result, probation and parole are used extensively. In 1965, slightly more than half of the offenders sentenced to correctional treatment were placed on probation, a total of 684,088 individuals. The annual cost of operating probation departments (felony and juvenile) is approximately $112,957,249.[14] The parole system is quite extensive although it is not as vast as probation. For the nation as a whole, more than 60 percent of adult felons are released on parole prior to the expiration of their sentences. In 1965 there were a total of 172,625 individuals on parole with an annual cost of $53,908,022.[15]

It is important to note that probation and parole do not constitute the totality of criminal rehabilitation in the United States. Half-way houses, therapy groups, and vocational guidance programs greatly increase correction statistics. Considering all programs for 1965, there were 1,282,386 offenders under correctional authority with a total of 121,163 employees attending them at a cost of $1,005,746,500 per year.[16] It has been estimated that by 1975 there will be a total of 1,841,000 individuals subjected to the rehabilitative efforts of society.[17]

Accompanying the tremendous effort and expenditures

involved in criminal rehabilitation is a vast body of theory relating to criminal etiology and treatment. An overview of the more popular theories will be presented in the next several pages.

B. THEORIES ON THE ETIOLOGY
OF CRIMINAL BEHAVIOR

1. Legalistic

The legalistic approach holds that criminology is obligated to function from the basis of statutory and judicial definitions of criminal acts. The criminal is defined in terms of his intent and act; for example, a robber is one who has been convicted of robbery, a murderer one convicted of murder, etc. Legal classifications represent the earliest and most commonly used categories in dealing with the criminal. The legalist's position is that adjudicated offenders represent the closest approximation of those who have violated the law. Legal classifications, however, do not preclude the study of offenders falling into legal categories and subcategories by behavioral scientists. Paul Tappan, a lawyer and sociologist, claimed that criminals are a sociologically distinct group who have violated specific legal norms and are subject to official state treatment. To him legal norms, their violation, and the mechanics of dealing with breach constitute major provinces of criminology.[18]

One must understand the definition of criminal law because it is vital in comprehending the nature of the legalistic approach. The criminal law is conventionally defined as a body of specific rules about human conduct which have been promulgated by political authority, which apply uniformly to all members of the classes to which the rules refer, and which are enforced by punishment administered by the state.[19] Hence, the criminal law is distinguishable from other bodies of rules by politicality, specificity, uniformity, and penal sanction.[20]

Politicality refers to the principle that activity can only be considered criminal if it is in violation of official rules made by the state. Specificity indicates that each prohibited act must be precisely defined (criminal law contains no general provision that any act which injures someone is a punishable offense). Uniformity implies that criminal behavior by any citizen, regardless of class or position, will invoke state sanction. Penal sanction refers to the notion that a violator will be punished, or threatened with punishment, by the state. Punishment for crime is to be imposed dispassionately by representatives of the state, and only in the interests of the state.[21]

Those who maintain a legalistic approach to criminology are generally aware of its shortcomings. The legalistic approach ignores criminal motivation and, in many cases, laws no longer supported by the broader values of the community remain on the books. Nevertheless, it is felt that the legalistic approach is needed as a basis or framework in the field of criminology, providing it is viewed in proper perspective.[22] The Supreme Court gives ample evidence of how law can be interpreted differently or even changed. Also, over periods of time, new laws must be enacted when needed. It must further be noted that laws differ from one geographical area to another.

2. Physical-Constitutional-Hereditary

The constitutional approach to crime has had few adherents in the United States since the early decades of the twentieth century. Neither the reported findings of the criminal anthropologists nor the constitutional studies of recent European criminal biologists have had much impact on American behavioral scientists in their study and classification of criminals.[23] The following representative approaches begin with Lombroso and end with recent constitutional studies.

Cesare Lombroso (1836-1909), a physician, was the leader of the school of thought known as the "Italian School."[24] The first statement of his theory was in the form of a pamphlet, published in 1876. It grew to a three-volume book in subsequent editions.[25] In its earlier form, this theory consisted of the following propositions.

(a) Criminals are by birth a distinct, asymmetrical type. (b) This type can be recognized by stigmata or anomalies such as an asymmetrical cranium, long lower jaw, flattened nose, scanty beard, and low sensitivity to pain. The criminal type is clearly represented in a person with more than five such stigmata, incompletely represented by three to five, and not necessarily indicated by less than three. (c) These physical anomalies do not in themselves cause crime but identify the personality predisposed to criminal behavior. This personality is either a reversion or atavism, or else a degeneration akin to epilepsy. (d) Because of their personal natures, such persons cannot refrain from crime unless the circumstances of life are unusually favorable. (e) It is often possible to classify what type of criminal an individual might become by considering his particular configuration of physical stigmata. Lombroso gradually modified his theory, however, and concluded that only 40 percent of criminals were "born" criminals, rather than the 100 percent he had originally believed.

Lombroso's theory was shattered when a British physician, Dr. Charles Goring, made a comparison of several thousand criminals and noncriminals and found no significant physical differences between them.[26] Although Lombroso's theory was no longer widely accepted after Goring's work, his physiological approach to criminal etiology continued to inspire certain researchers. The general body-build, or somatotype, received considerable attention. William Sheldon found three somatotypes and attributed psychological characteristics to each. The endomorph has a round, soft body and is quite concerned with relaxation, food, and affection. The mesomorph is round and hard, likes adventure and is concerned with domination and aggression. The third body type, the ectomorph, has a thin, fragile body and prefers privacy, pensive activities, and emotional restraint. Sheldon classified somatotypes by assigning a numerical value to various physical traits. By doing so, he believed that an individual could be classified, not only physically, but mentally. Sheldon then proceeded to relate the various personality types with predispositions toward the commission of specific crimes.[27] Sheldon was not the first to attribute personality to body structure. Ernest Kretschmer had earlier designated three somatotypes: asthenic, athletic, and pyknic. Each somatotype was predisposed to a certain mental orientation. Pyknics (similar to Sheldon's endomorph) were generally cyclic personality types or manic-depressive, if psychotic. The asthenic (ectomorph) and athletic (mesomorph) were associated with introversion and schizophrenia. The Gluecks also followed the somatotype approach to crime and compiled a book *Physique and Delinquency*, which reported a high incidence of mesomorphs among delinquents. More important, from a typological frame of reference, they concluded that different cultural stresses produce different patterns of response for each of four body types.[28]

Other scientists, employing a physiological approach to criminal etiology, have emphasized the role of the endocrine glands in causing criminal behavior. Edward Podolsky claimed that certain offense types can be associated with specific glandular dysfunctions.[29] Berman suggests that there are various endocrine types of personality in which one or another of the hormones may connote the pattern of an individual's behavior.[30] Although certain investigators have found relationships between glandular dysfunctions and criminal behavior, the evidence is not yet conclusive.

Two Boston neurosurgeons have found that, in some cases, erratic and agressive behavior can be traced to brain damage. In many of their patients, brain damage was not obvious. Examinations in depth, however, revealed abnormal brain tissue. The affected tissue could have been congenital, the result of blows to the head, or of some viral infection that reached the brain.[31] There has been evidence that many violent criminals possess an abnormal "XYY" chromosome. Improper chromosomal structure or various sorts of brain damage apparently leave the affected areas in an abnormally excitable electrical state so that impulses of rage and violence can be triggered on almost any provocation.[32] For example, a man driving to work may suddenly be enraged because another driver cut him off too sharply and then go to excessive lengths in order to get even. Certain EEG studies indicate that the persistent delinquent with serious aggressive behavior problems may vary neurologically from "normals." Daniel Silverman did electroencephalographic studies on criminal psychopaths and found that 80 percent of his subjects had abnormal or borderline tracings.[33] George Thompson found 280 severe delinquents to have a significantly higher rate of neurological abnormalities than 100 controls.[34]

The Physical Constitutional-Hereditary approach to criminal etiology has had adherents, both past and contemporary. Although much of their research has been thought-provoking, sufficient evidence to relate criminal behavior with biology has not been produced in most cases. Theories attributing crime to the "mental defective" or the physiologically abnormal have not been comprehensive enough to explain the "exceptions to the rule." Nevertheless, all forms of research in criminal etiology are needed and will have to be encouraged if society hopes to isolate and eradicate criminal behavior.

3. Psychological

The development of psychology in the last five decades stimulated the application of psychological techniques to the problems of crime. The publication of *The Individual Delinquent* by William Healy in 1915 signaled the liberation of psychology from Lombrosian preconceptions and opened the way for research and theory about crime that has profoundly influenced criminological thought. [35]

The central thesis of the psychological school is that a certain organization of the personality, developed entirely apart from criminal culture, will result in criminal behavior regardless of social situation. The individual motivated toward crime, according to this school, has a psychological disorder which if identified can often be treated. The more extreme writers hold that almost all criminals have abnormal personalities; the less extreme writers attempt to isolate a smaller fraction of criminals for this type of explanation. This latter group appears to merge somewhat with the sociological school.

The early preoccupation of psychologists and psychiatrists was with the assumption that criminals constitute an inferior type, characterized by feeblemindedness, mental disease, alcholism, drug addiction, psychopathy, neuroticism, and the like. In early attempts to prove these contentions statistically, research procedure was often faulty and operational definitions were vague. This was true of such concepts as "constitutional psychopath," "inadequate personality," and the like.[36] In addition to the diagnosis of serious mental defects and disorders, there has been a trend toward the enumeration of all kinds of personality traits related to criminal behavior. The assumption is that a normal, well-balanced personality possesses adequate mental and emotional equipment and that the absence of such equipment may lead to various forms of deviant behavior, crime included. Psychologists are to some extent abandoning their efforts to demonstrate the prevalence of deviations from the normal among criminals in favor of describing the processes involved in the development of criminal mentality. By the use of intensive case studies, they emphasize the relationship between repressed conflicts, early traumas, especially those connected with sex, and other motivations, and the onset of criminal behavior.[37] The number of psychological theories pertaining to criminal etiology is enormous. Not only do they vary widely in scope and approach, they are often contradictory. Psychiatrists and psychologists seem to approach the problem of motivation by categorizing the type of crime committed. For example, sex offenders have a different personality than do armed robbers. Drug-users differ psychologically from white-collar offenders. Although attempts have been made at classifying criminals into major personality types, according to their behavioral patterns, there is seldom total agreement on the part of experts involved.[38] Nevertheless, several plausible theories have been advanced concerning the psychological basis of criminal behavior.

John Dollard advanced a theory purporting to explain violent behavior. His frustration-aggression hypothesis states that, if an individual is frustrated in his attempt to reach a certain goal, violence will often be his reaction.

This violence, however, is not necessarily directed at the individual or institution which originally blocked the goal-directed behavior. The frustrated individual will generally vent his agression on an object which will not, or cannot, retaliate to any extensive degree.[39]

Various psychologists consider narcotics addiction to be the result of an inadequately developed personality. The drug-dependent person is described as abnormally passive and immature. Furthermore, he is female-dependent and lacks adequate male identification. Isolation and anomie are also characteristic of the personality of the narcotics addict. The euphoria and escape from reality offered by opiates enable such an individual to survive in what he considers to be a hostile world.[40] Because this escape is what the narcotics addict needs so much, he seldom views his addiction as problematic and will often resist treatment.

Karl Abraham, a psychoanalyst, attributed prostitution to a lack of sexuality in the prostitute herself. He argued that a woman who cannot enjoy sex with a single partner feels compelled to change partners constantly. Through this form of compensation, the prostitute avenges herself on every man by demonstrating that the sex act, so important to him, means little to her. She is thus unconsciously or even consciously humiliating all men by having intercourse with any and all customers. Frank Caprio carried this idea about lack of heterosexuality in the prostitute to its zenith by arguing that prostitution is primarily a defense mechanism against homosexual desires. These desires are so strong that they force the woman to make every attempt to repudiate them.[41]

A monumental study of American prostitutes was done by Harold Greenwald. His subjects were call girls who occupy the top of their profession and earn an average of $20,000 per year. He found them to be charming and able to maintain fairly intelligent conversations. Not out of line with previous ideas, Greenwald found that the primary predisposing factor in the prostitutes' backgrounds was a history of severe maternal deprivation. This loss of the mother's love caused them to turn increasingly to their father for affection, but usually the father failed to give the necessary emotional support. This led the prostitutes to turn to self-debasement and the search for security, warmth, and love through prostitution. The primary psychological mechanisms used by the women were projection, denial, and reaction-formation.[42]

Classic psychoanalytical theories of criminal etiology generally deal with conflicts with the id. In the psycho-analyst's scheme, the human personality is composed of three parts: the primitive, animal id; the ego, or total personality; and the superego, the socially determined "conscience." Some writers on psychoanalysis have made the unresolved conflicts between the primitive, instinctive drives of the id and the requirements of the social superego to be almost synonymous with criminal behavior. Accord-ing to this view, crime arises out of the failure of socialization to adequately control the savage and animal nature of man. Criminal behavior is thought of as an almost necessary outcome of an uncontrolled personality. Thus, the criminal need not be related to any "criminal" culture. More extreme psychoanalysts hold that the only difference between the criminal and the normal man is that the normal man has found ways to vent his aggression in a socially acceptable manner whereas the criminal has not.[43]

The theories just presented by no means cover the breadth and scope of psychological explanations of criminal behavior. To any number of crimes there exist any number of psychological theories. The foregoing ideas were discussed in order to exemplify the type of approach taken by members of the psychological school. It should be noted that attempts to explain criminal behavior on a purely psychological basis are giving way to a more eclectic approach. It is becoming apparent that an overwhelming majority of criminals fall within a normal personality range. The field of sociology has made several contribu-tions to the understanding of criminal etiology and behavior. It is to these sociological theories that we now turn.

4. Sociological

The sociological approach to criminal etiology emphasizes the relationship between social and cultural conditions and crime. The central theme of the sociological school holds that crime and criminality are products of the same social processes that produce other kinds of social behavior. Perhaps the most important theory of criminal behavior yet advanced is the theory of "differential association."

According to Sutherland and Cressey, an individual develops a pattern of criminal behavior because he is socialized to do so. That is, criminal behavior is learned through interaction with other persons in a process of communication. The principal part of the learning includes (a) techniques of committing crime and (b) the specific direction of motives, drive, rationalizations, and attitudes. The specific direction of motives and drives is learned from definitions of the legal codes as favorable or unfavorable. An individual becomes delinquent if he holds an excess of definitions favorable to violation of the law over definitions unfavorable to violation of the law. When persons become criminal, they do so because of contacts with criminal patterns and relative isolation from noncriminal patterns. This is the principle of "differential association." These associations may vary in frequency, duration, priority, and intensity. Such factors would have a bearing on the individual's subsequent criminal pattern. It is further noted by Sutherland and Cressey that the process of learning criminal behavior involves all of the mechanisms that are involved in any other learning. While criminal behavior is an expression of needs and values, it is not explained by these needs and values since noncriminal behavior can be an expression of the same needs and values.[44]

Many forms of criminal behavior are learned and not the result of a certain personality structure which automatically leads the individual into deviant behavior. As we have noted, in psychological theories on prostitution, the prostitute is viewed as an unstable personality seeking the warmth and security denied her in early childhood. The sociological school would hold, however, that the personality of the prostitute falls in the normal range. The deciding factor is her history of learning experiences. That is, the prostitute learned to define prostitution as an acceptable alternate form of enterprise. She experiences no immense degree of guilt or frustration. This is not to say that she may not wish to change her profession, but she is able to live with it.[45]

Although the theory of differential association advanced by Sutherland is widely accepted, sociologists have investigated criminal etiology from other perspectives. In a stable society, the majority of individuals conform to cultural goals and accept institutional means for achieving them. However, when there is great emphasis upon success goals, without equal emphasis on the means for achieving them, individual adaptations may vary greatly. Merton found five types of adaptation to a social structure which emphasizes the same cultural goals for all but denies many the legitimate means necessary for accomplishing these goals. The innovator accepts the goals but does not employ normative means to achieve the goal, e.g., the robber-barons of the nineteenth century. The ritualist accepts the means but does not accept the goals, thus sparing himself psychological strain should he be unable to actually achieve these goals, e.g., the misfeasant bureaucrat. The rebel is characterized by a combination of rejection and acceptance both of social goals and means for achieving them, e.g., the revolutionary who would destroy and rebuild a society. The retreatist withdraws from society altogether, rejecting the goals and the means, e.g., the addict. Finally, there is the conformist, who accepts both the goals and the means for achieving them.[46]

Albert Cohen investigated delinquent gangs of boys and offered a theory purporting to explain their often violent and aggressive behavior. Essentially, Cohen believes that lower-class delinquent gangs do not hold middle-class values because these values are not always functional in their world. Consequently, these boys do not mirror middle-class people and the things they stand for, such as ambition, self-reliance, delayed gratification, and good manners. When lower-class boys fail to display such behavior, they are often rebuffed by members of the middle class, such as teachers, who consider them to be of low status. This causes resentment and hostility. The subculture which the boys form is the opposite of and hostile to middle-class values and is characterized by short-run hedonism, versatility in certain types of delinquent behavior, and group autonomy from social control other than that imposed by the gang itself. Miller, on the other hand, views lower-class culture and behavior as autonomous and independent of middle-class culture. According to his theory, delinquents are not reacting against the middle class but, instead, they are following distinctive lower-class traditions.[47]

Cloward and Ohlin, continuing in the tradition of Merton and Cohen, have explained the existence of delinquent subcultures through a theory of conflict between values which promote unlimited aspirations and a social structure which restricts accomplishment of these aspirations. Among some segments of the population, the possibilities of achieving even limited success in a legitimate fashion are restricted. As a form of adaption to such a situation, three types of delinquent subcultures provide avenues to success goals. In the "criminal subculture," wealth can be obtained through thievery, extortion, fraud, etc. In the "conflict subculture," achievement of status relates to force and the manipulation of force. The third subculture is retreatist and contains definitions favoring the consumption of drugs. Cloward and Ohlin believe these subcultures persist because younger adolescents become socialized by older members of the subcultures. The conflict subculture is less persistent due to the fact that conflict often becomes less functional as an individual matures.[48]

There have been other theories of criminal etiology which, although not necessarily restricted to the realm of sociology, have been examined by various sociologists over the decades. For example, the cartographic or geographic school of criminology held that crime was a function of climate and cultural conditions. That is, circum-mediterranean peoples were more disposed to crimes of passion than were nordic peoples. The Socialist school believed crime was an outcome of the conflict between the proletariat and the bourgeoisie. These theories, however, eventually lost popularity due to their inability to account for the overwhelming number of cases which did not fall within their scope.

The sociological theories of criminal etiology discussed herein do not represent the thinking of the entire school. A variety of sociological theories can be found to explain many different kinds of criminal behavior. Nevertheless, most such theories look to the subculture and peer groups of the deviant individual for an explanation of his criminal behavior.

In recent years, scholars in the fields of sociology and psychology have been increasingly willing to listen to the views of one another. Current theories of criminal etiology have made an attempt to incorporate the findings of both sociology and psychology. This synthesis is apparent in theories on criminal rehabilitation. As will be seen in the following section, the deviant individual must be perceived as both a psychological and sociological entity if any form of criminal rehabilitation is to take place.

C. PROCESS AND THEORIES OF CRIMINAL REHABILITATION

1. Choice of Milieu

The first step in the process of rehabilitation involves selection of the milieu in which the criminal is to be treated. This decision is usually left to the presiding judge who, considering the recommendations of probation investigators, clinicians, and other interested parties, must decide whether the convict is to be treated while in custody or while a resident in the community. Such a decision, of course, would require at least a preliminary diagnosis of the individual's psychological and social condition. Theoretically, rehabilitation will take place in the community if it is decided that his presence there does not constitute a threat to life and property. If preliminary diagnosis reveals that he is not yet capable of refraining from criminal behavior, the individual will be placed in custody until such time as his sentence expires or he is considered capable of law-abiding behavior. Custodial supervision can range anywhere from incarceration in a prison to mandatory residence at a half-way house where the individual is allowed daily supervised movement in the community. In those instances where the individual is not considered to pose a threat to the community, he is generally released on probation and his activities are monitored and directed by the probation officer assigned to the case. This book is not the place for a detailed analysis of the various types of rehabilitation programs in effect today. Nevertheless, it can be said that the major distinction between programs is whether the subject is in a constantly controlled environment or whether he remains a member of the community.

2. Diagnosis

It may seem strange that diagnosis often takes place after the individual has been placed in a selected milieu. Normally, however, diagnosis is a continual process influenced by feedback from the individual's behavior. Before the criminal is sentenced by the presiding judge, the judge often has a report on the subject's sociological and psychological status. This diagnosis, however, is generally brief and introductory or, in many cases, no diagnosis is made at all. This is due to the poor financial resources of the courts and to the overwhelming number of cases referred annually to clinics and probation departments. Once placement has been made, however, the criminal is subjected to more extensive evaluation, particularly if he is on probation or in a half-way house.[49] An individual's criminal behavior is generally diagnosed as stemming from his psychological state of mind or from his social environment. Naturally, there is a tremendous overlap between these two factors. It is for this reason that treatment of the criminal involves not only a psychological but a sociological approach. As examples, we shall investigate more thoroughly two types of criminal behavior: the narcotics addict, who hurts primarily himself; and the thief, whose crimes are generally directed at the property of others. The narcotics addict is generally considered to have an inadequate personality. Due to factors in his childhood and adolescence, he is unable to face the pressures of life and relies on the euphoria of narcotics in order to escape responsibility. Although he often steals to support his habit, his primary victim is himself.[50] If he were provided with free narcotics, he would probably cease thievery but would continue to withdraw from reality. Such an individual has a severe psychological problem and is generally subjected to psychotherapy or group therapy.[51]

On the other hand, the thief often exhibits no psychological abnormality. He steals because he has defined such behavior as a personally acceptable manner in which to obtain money. Although he generally realizes that he is technically committing a crime, the socialization process has equipped him with a series of rationalizations. He may believe that he has no choice but to steal, that he is merely "paying someone back," that he is not really stealing but taking what is owed him, or that he is otherwise justified in what he is doing.[52] The reason for his crimes can often be traced to his values and attitudes. Treatment of a thief of this type would involve the replacement of his frame-of-reference with one more acceptable to society as a whole.

3. Treatment

Theoretically, curing the narcotics addict is merely a matter of finding something that will interest him more than the thing he is addicted to. It must be realized from the onset of therapy that an addict rarely has a two-way relationship with anybody. He may become attached to someone he can lean on, a girlfriend for instance, but this is the kind of attachment an infant has for his mother. He loves her for what she does for him, not for herself. In this way, as in many other ways, addicts are childlike in their emotional behavior. This gives a clue to one method of curing the addict—by getting him to form a more stable relationship with another person.[53] This can sometimes be accomplished by a skillful therapist who can guide the patient into realizing his motivations and desires.

Curing the addict is a two-stage process. First, the addiction of the body has to be arrested. This is to say that the addict must stop taking the drug, recover from the withdrawal effects, and clear his brain of any mind-altering effects of the drug. This makes it possible for his ego to engage in the second part, which is to find something which will interest him more than narcotics. Some addicts can decide to stop taking the drug all by themselves, but most need the strength and encouragement provided by a clinician or a group of concerned people. Once the addict is without the drug, he can begin to look objectively at his situation. At this point, the therapist helps him notice that his life seems empty and that he does not really love anybody, not even himself. Although he thinks of himself as a "great lover" and possibly a sociable person, his relationship with people tends to be twisted or unpleasant. He attaches himself to people because he needs them and uses them as props for his weakness. Thus, the second part of the treatment involves helping the addict see people in a different light, as ends themselves rather than means to an end.

Helping the addict to substitute people for drugs can best be accomplished in a treatment group where the people that the addict needs are right in front of him. Treatment, however, is likely to take at least a year or so. Psychotherapy should be supported by other ways of getting the addict to look at himself and, eventually, to like what he sees. Technical training and an opportunity to counsel other narcotics addicts in their attempt to "kick the habit" are useful techniques.[54] Treating the thief whose criminal activity seems to result from his membership in a particular subculture requires a somewhat different approach. Theoretically, a successful rehabilitation program is based on the need to remove the subject from adherence to the values of his subculture, establish a different kind of culture, and win the cooperation that stems from a real desire to change. The first step is to establish contact with the subject when he is under stress. In a prison situation, he could be in solitary confinement. If on probation, the subject might be suffering pressures from friends and family because he is not contributing to their support. The rehabilitation worker attempts to extricate him from his predicament, but with the continuing admonishment that "something has to change." In continuing talks with the thief, the worker points out to him the factors in his life and subculture which led to his incarceration or probation sentence. Once the subject actually understands this, the worker induces him to transfer identity from his subculture to the worker himself. This switchover is reinforced with appropriate rewards: special privileges, greater freedom, and trust. Without this reinforcement of approved behavior, transference of identity would be meaningless.

The subject must also realize that his acceptance of prescribed behavioral patterns will prove useful in other than therapeutic situations. To accomplish this, he should be guided into activities aimed at improving his social and vocational abilities. Standard courtesy and manners should be reinforced whenever possible, as should interest in any vocation of the individual's choosing. Vocational training, however, should be subtly encouraged rather than forced.

We have discussed two examples of criminal rehabilitation programs. The former is highly psychological in that it aims at personality change. The latter is highly sociological due to its effort at reconstructing the values and subculture to which the individual adheres. These two examples have also shown the degree of interrelationship psychology and sociology must bring to bear on the problem of criminal rehabilitation. No psychological function can be separated from the individual's social milieu, just as no social interaction can take place without somehow affecting the personality of the individual. To further exemplify the multidisciplinary approach employed by the field of criminal rehabilitation, we turn to the work of Don Gibbons.

4. A Working Typology

Diagnosis, classification, and treatment of criminal offenders have been discussed extensively by Don Gibbons, a sociologist primarily concerned with crime and delinquency.[55] He asserts that effective treatment can only be realized through complete understanding of the motives, personality, and criminal patterns of the offender. To this end, he has composed a criminal typology which considers the psychological and sociological circumstances of different types of offenders, as well as appropriate therapeutic approaches to each criminal type.[56] The following is a highly abridged report on his findings:

I. *Professional Thief*, defined as the offender who participates in a highly skilled nonviolent form of crime, including confidence games, shoplifting, pocket-picking, and other kinds of professional thievery. Very few are found in prison because of their cleverness in avoiding arrest. These occupational types have frequent contacts with the underworld. Proposed treatment—group therapy, along with a systematic frustration of "con-politician" behavior. Longer sentences are also recommended. Parole planning should guide this type of offender toward law-abiding occupations employing their verbal skills.

II. *Professional "Heavy" Criminal*, defined as the offender who engages in highly skilled, full-time, lucrative, property crime, i.e., armed robbery, burglary, and other direct assaults upon property. These criminal activities are carried on as a team or mob operation. Professional heavies define themselves as professional criminals and are satisfied with their criminal life-style. Proposed treatment—no specific treatment is advocated. Fortunately, according to Gibbons, professionals ultimately reform themselves by retiring from criminality because at a certain age they decide the hazards of crime are too great.

III. *Semiprofessional Property Criminal*, defined as the offender who tries to carry on crime as an occupation despite limited criminal skills. Such criminals engage in armed robbery, hold-ups, burglaries, larcenies, and direct assaults upon personal or private property. They view themselves as victims of a corrupt society in which all occupational roles constitute rackets. As "system blamers," they relieve themselves of guilt feelings. Proposed treatment—intensive group therapy in the various correctional institutions, probation treatment with small caseloads centering around group therapy, compulsory involvement in group therapy in prison, concentrated group therapy treatment immediately prior to release from prison, halfway houses, etc.

IV. *Property Offender "One-Time Loser"*, defined as the unskilled loner without previous delinquent or criminal record who commits a single, serious property crime. Such offenders are often arrested and placed on probation. They are prosocial in attitude and for the most part have lived conventional, law-abiding lives. They identify themselves as noncriminals. Proposed treatment—probation with minimal supervision: those institutionalized should be confined in minimum security correctional facilities and isolated from offenders with criminalistic attitudes.

V. *Automobile Thief and Joyrider*, defined as the adult version of the delinquent type. Most members of this category who are incarcerated succeed on parole and henceforth lead law-abiding lives.

VI. *Naive Check Forger*, defined as an unsophisticated, recidivistic check passer without delinquent history or otherwise criminal background. These offenders do not define themselves as criminals and attempt to rationalize away their offenses as minor infractions. Proposed treatment—group therapy to build up a fund of acceptable solutions to problems which these offenders have thus far responded to by writing checks; "shock therapy" in terms of a jail or institutional commitment early in their check-passing careers.

VII. *White-Collar Criminal*, defined as a person in business and corporate organizations who violates state and federal regulatory statutes. They are normal, conventional people who learn definitions favorable to the violation of the law in their everyday business activities. They define themselves as law-abiding citizens. Proposed treatment—vigorous and consistent law enforcement is recommended. Regulatory agencies should ferret out these violators and stiff fines and prison sentences levied.

VIII. *Professional Fringe Violator*, defined as a member of a legitimate profession who utilizes professional skills in the commission of crimes, e.g., doctors who perform abortions. They regard themselves as law-abiding citizens and not as criminals. They begin their illegal acts late in life, are infrequently detected or prosecuted. Proposed treatment—no treatment per se is recommended, because these offenders are normal and prosocial.

IX. *Embezzler*, defined as an offender who violates a position of trust by stealing large sums of money from employers, usually through alteration of business records. They build up rationalizations that they were only borrowing the money, etc. They possess prosocial attitudes and do not have delinquent or criminal records. Embezzlers are products of respectable middle-class backgrounds. Proposed treatment—no treatment is required for these normals. In penal institutions they should be isolated from contacts with more criminalistic inmates.

X. *Personal Offender, "One-Time Loser"*, defined as an offender involved in a serious, violent crime. Frequently, these violent acts are "victim precipitated," and involve spouses, etc. Long term tension and antagonism between perpetrator and victim usually precede the criminal assault. Proposed treatment—no treatment is recommended for these normals. In prison they should be segregated from antisocial inmates. They require help from parole officers upon release.

XI. *Psychopathic Assaulter*, defined as the adult counterpart of the delinquent pattern of the Overly Aggressive Delinquent. Such offenders are members of a recidivistic group of offenders who commit a variety of offenses against property and persons. Proposed treatment—Gibbons recommends that these offenders be incarcerated in specialized institutions.

XII. *Violent Sex Offender*, defined as offender who violently attacks female victims. The assaults are characterized by extreme and bizarre violence, often culminating in homicide. Family backgrounds are characterized by a family pattern of repressive sexual notions, seductive mother-son relationships, etc. Proposed treatment—Gibbons recommends psychotherapy.

XIII. *Nonviolent Sex Offender*, defined as the offender involved in exhibitionism, child-molesting, or incest where violence is seldom employed. They define themselves as noncriminals. Proposed treatment—client-centered therapy, individual psychotherapy, and group therapy.

XIV. *Nonviolent Sex Offender—Statutory Rape*, defined as adult males who participate in sexual intercourse with minor females. They exhibit prosocial attitudes, and do not have previous records of delinquency or crime. Proposed treatment—no treatment is recommended. Probation rather than incarceration is indicated.

XV. *Narcotics Addict*, defined as "double failures" whose

dependent and insecure personalities preclude membership in either a prosocial or delinquent group. Proposed
treatment—Gibbons recommends for this group treatment akin to that suggested for juvenile narcotics
users—long-term milieu management patterned after
Synanon.[57]

Certainly Gibbons' typological scheme is open to
criticism for errors of omission and commission. Nevertheless, his typology represents one of the most systematic
and plausible classifications to date. Particularly laudable is
his inclusion of both psychological and sociological
perspectives. Such a synthesis is the goal long sought after
by most schools of thought. There are still questions,
however, regarding the actual implementation and degree
of success of the various approaches to criminal
rehabilitation.

D. AN ANALYSIS OF CRIMINAL REHABILITATION

The effects of behavior intervention in the criminolegal
systems seem hard to measure. There are a number of
differing opinions and volumes of contradictory empirical
data regarding the efficacy of criminal rehabilitation.
Supervision in the community in the form of probation
and parole is becoming a favored correctional alternative,
yet the ability to accurately predict success eludes us. Karl
Schuessler has indicated that parole prediction, notwithstanding the vigorous attempts of social scientists, is still
far from reliable.[58] Not only is it difficult to predict
probation-parole outcome, but the factors which spell
success or failure are difficult to isolate.

It has long been assumed that the more personal
supervision a probation or parole officer can give a client,
the smaller the chance of recidivism. Theoretically, the
probation or parole officer acts as liaison between the
convicted individual and society. Because of his knowledge
of community resources, government offices, and job
sources, the rehabilitation worker is in a position to
provide a number of occupational, vocational, and medical
services to his client. Not only does the worker provide

objective services, he relates on a personal basis to the client and his family. Through a series of home visits, probation and parole officers come to know more of the psychological and sociological pressures under which the client is attempting to function. Where more extensive counseling or therapy seems appropriate, psychiatric care can often be arranged. Thus, through personal and supportive services, extensive contact between worker and client is expected to reduce recidivism. This was the case in the Saginaw Probation Demonstration Project of 1963. Under the auspices of the Michigan Crime and Delinquency Council, the Saginaw County Probation Department gave increased supervision to an experimental group of probationers. Because of his reduced caseload, each probation officer was able to spend more time in the presentence investigation, counseling, and supervision of each subject. The results of the three-year study indicated that increased supervision resulted in a greater degree of resocialization. The control group (N-170) had 42.2 percent of its members committed to fail for violation of probation. The experimental group (N-102) had a violation rate of just 31.2 percent.[59]

A more recent study in California indicated that there was no significant relationship between amount of supervision and recidivism. San Francisco probation authorities assessed probationers under three types of supervision caseloads: minimum supervision (one contact a month); ideal supervision (not less than two contacts a month); and intensive supervision (not less than four contacts a month). During a two-year period, the violation rates were 22.2 percent for minimum supervision subjects, 24.3 percent for ideal, and 37.5 for those in the intensive group. Since the intensive supervision group may have had more technical violations due to the fact that their behavior was more closely scrutinized than the other two groups, a further computation was made. Excluding technical violations, the violation rates were 22.2 percent (N-118) for minimum supervision; 22 percent (N-119) for ideal supervision, and 20.0 percent (N-70) for intensive supervision. The difference in recidivism was not significant.[60]

Contradictory studies such as the Saginaw and San Francisco projects cannot be easily explained. One could look to gross errors in research design but such an explanation would probably prove fruitless. Moreover, the excessive number of contradictory studies weighs against such a line of thought.

Some corrections workers believe that optimum rehabilitation can only take place through a total community approach. The Midcity project carried out in Boston between 1954 and 1957 produced evidence against this assumption. The community segment of this program involved two major parts. Local citizens' groups were encouraged to discourage juvenile gang activities in their neighborhoods. In addition, increased cooperation among various agencies was effected. Churches, schools, police, and probation departments carried out an intensive and coordinated campaign against delinquent behavior in a selected district. A number of families in the area with long records of dependency were given an intensive dose of psychiatric casework. Furthermore, professional social workers dealt with delinquent gangs using the detached-worker strategem. At the end of the designated three-year period, the project failed to achieve a significant reduction in delinquency.[61]

Certain rehabilitation programs aimed at reintegrating the individual offender into a prosocial community have claimed success. In 1965, a nonprofit corporation named Job Therapy, Inc., was chartered in the state of Washington. The program called for the assignment of a volunteer sponsor to a jailed inmate who is to be released within a year. The sponsor visits him monthly and tries to gain his confidence. Each sponsor signs a pledge that he will escort his charge from the institution and remain with him throughout his first day in free society. The sponsor is also pledged to assist with any problems of re-entry into the community. Coupled with this personal attention is the promise of a job. Employers and neighbors are contacted, interviewed, and asked to aid in the resocialization of the subject. The program's director, as well as high state officials, consider Job Therapy, Inc., to be a complete success. So far, they claim to have matched 500 reputable volunteers with almost 600 confined men. In May, 1970, 77 out of 90 parolees were placed in suitable jobs and demonstrated ostensibly prosocial attitudes.

The amount of rehabilitation which takes place within the confines of a prison seems to be nil, according to certain prison officials. Gus Harrison, Director of Corrections for the state of Michigan, has stated that even the best prison systems will have limited success.[62] After extensive interviews with members of the Connecticut Parole Board, one magazine concluded that "Prisons remain academies of bitterness and frustration rather than rehabilitation."[63] The argument against effective rehabilitation in a prison setting seems twofold: first, incarceration with seriously antisocial offenders tends to harden and frustrate more socially adjusted inmates and, second, it is impossible to gear a man for life in a freer society while he is in a restricted environment. Nevertheless, some prison officials report a high degree of success for prison programs. Project First Change, operated by the South Carolina Department of Corrections, provides basic education, job placement, and social services for the inmates and their families, and offers environmental and psychological support in the form of a "halfway house." The effectiveness of the program was measured by comparing and analyzing various inmates according to the degree of participation in the program. Results showed that nearly twice as many members of the control group—those who had not participated in the program—returned to prison, and significantly more graduates of the program than nongraduates held jobs.[64]

It may never be possible to reconcile the disparity between those projects which show evidence of success and those which do not. Taking a broader view of the entire scope of criminal rehabilitation, however, may result in firmer conclusions. As stated earlier, the very existence of recidivism implies failure of the criminological institution to provide an effective program of behavior intervention. Theoretically, the greater the degree of recidivism, the greater the degree of failure. During the past ten years, the quality of prisons and correctional personnel has greatly improved. The public has taken note of deplorable conditions in many prisons, jails, and workhouses and has pressed for reform. Although there remains much to be done, facilities and penal practices are becoming more sophisticated. Correctional workers themselves have become more educated and knowledgeable. Most probation and parole officers, as well as prison counselors, are required to have at least a college degree in a social science. Furthermore, psychiatric-psychological treatment and other therapeutic services are becoming more and more available to subjects in correctional systems. Nevertheless, recidivism rates do not appear to have changed. Conrad reports a study of 2959 men released from institutions (after having been "rehabilitated") in 1954. Six years later, nearly 2/3 had been reconvicted.[65] As part of a federal "Careers in Crime" research program, the recidivism rates of 18,567 offenders released to the community in 1963 were examined. The study revealed that 65 percent had been rearrested by the end of the sixth year after release. Of those persons who were arrested within the first year, but who were acquitted or had their cases dismissed, 92 percent were rearrested for new offenses. Of those released on probation, 57 percent repeated; parole, 63 percent; and mandatory release after serving prison time, 76 percent. [66]

From 1960 to 1969, violent crimes in the United States increased ten times as fast as the population. Violent crime went up 131 percent, whereas the population increased only 13 percent.[67] In 1963, there was approximately one murder every hour. In 1969, there was one every 36 minutes. There was one forcible rape every 32 minutes in 1963; in 1969, there was one every 14 minutes. There were 12 robberies an hour in 1963 compared to 30 per hour in 1969.[68] This increase in violent crime has been blamed on such things as increased poverty, discrimination, moral decay, and the war in Vietnam. Considering the fact that 75 percent of serious crime (assault, robbery, rape, murder, etc.) is committed by recidivists, it is also possible that the rate of recidivism may even be climbing. This determination cannot be made, however, until more sophisticated techniques and further studies are forthcoming.

Probably the greatest disparity in opinions is between

those which are expressed publicly and those expressed privately. Few corrections agencies will state that they are unable to effectively rehabilitate the criminal offender. On the contrary, they will often select and publish case histories of those individuals who seem to have been resocialized. On a private basis, however, many workers will concede that they find it difficult to intervene successfully in the behavior of their clients. This sort of admission is becoming more widely expressed. Appearing more often in professional journals, in juxtaposition to articles describing effective rehabilitation programs, are statements such as the following: "Despite our best efforts and intentions, we continue to be unsuccessful in the development of a scientifically valid correctional process."[69]

FOOTNOTES

1. J. Edgar Hoover, *Crime in the United States*, Uniform Crime Reports—1969 (Washington, D. C.: Federal Bureau of Investigation, 1970), p. 39.
2. These rates must be considered in light of the fact that Negroes and Indian Americans, due to their social visibility and vulnerable position in American society, are more liable to be arrested on suspicion alone.
3. David Dressler, *Practice and Theory of Probation and Parole* (2nd ed.; New York: Columbia University Press, 1969), pp. 152-158.
4. *loc. cit.*
5. One out of five robberies in Washington, D.C. was solved. Statement of Mr. Edward Bennett Williams, attorney-at-law, in *U. S. News and World Report*, March 16, 1970, p. 20.
6. Thomas Blight, "Recidivism," *Encyclopedia Britannica*, XIX (1965), p. 12.
7. *Detroil News*, Thursday, March 12, 1970, p. 20A.
8. "Crime Expense Now Up to 51 Billions a Year," *U. S. News and World Report*, October 26, 1970, p. 31.
9. *ibid.*, p. 30.
10. "More Aid for Cities in War Against Crime," *U. S. News and World Report*, February 23, 1970, p. 37
11. Dressler, *op. cit.*, pp. 16-20.
12. Lewis Diana, "What is Probation?" in *Probation and Parole: Selected Readings*, ed. by Robert M. Carter and Leslie T. Wilkins (New York: John Wiley & Sons, Inc., 1970), p. 40.
13. Charles L. Newman, *Sourcebook on Probation, Parole and Pardons* (Springfield: Charles C. Thomas, 1968), pp. 17-37.
14. The President's Commission on Law Enforcement and

Administration of Justice, *Task Force Report: Corrections* (Washington, D. C.: U. S. Government Printing Office, 1967), p. 27.

15. *ibid.*, p. 60.
16. *ibid.*, p. 1.
17. *ibid.*, p. 7.
18. Paul W. Tappan, "Who is the Criminal," *American Sociological Review*, XII (February, 1947), pp. 96-102.
19. Donald R. Cressey, "Crime" in *Contemporary Social Problems,* ed. by Robert K. Merton and Robert A. Nisbet (New York: Harcourt, Brace & World, Inc., 1961), p. 25.
20. Civil litigation nowhere implies incarceration. This is not true in criminal cases.
21. Cressey, *op. cit.,* p. 25.
22. Indeed, omitting the legal approach to criminology would be both a theoretical and practical impossibility.
23. Julian B. Roebuck, *Criminal Typology* (Springfield: Charles C. Thomas Co, 1967), p. 31.
24. *loc. cit.*
25. This early book is Cesare Lombroso, *L'Uomo Delinquente* (Torino: Bocca, 1896-97). See Edwin H. Sutherland and Donald R. Cressey, *Principles of Criminology* (7th ed.; New York: J. B. Lippincott Company, 1966), pp. 56-57.
26. Charles Goring, *The English Convict* (London: His Majesty's Stationery Office, 1913), pp. 99-100.
27. William H. Sheldon, *Varieties of Delinquent Youth: An Introduction to Constitutional Psychiatry* (New York: Harper and Brothers, 1949).
28. Sheldon and Eleanor Glueck, *Physique and Delinquency* (New York: Harper and Brothers, 1956), pp. 161-273.
29. Edward Podolsky, "The Chemical Brew of Criminal Behavior," *Journal of Criminal Law, Criminology and Police Science,* VL (March/April, 1955), pp. 675-678.
30. Louis Berman, "Crime and the Endocrine Glands," *American Journal of Psychiatry,* XII (September, 1932), pp. 215-238.
31. Albert Rosenfeld, "The Psycho-biology of Violence," *Life,* June 21, 1968, p. 69.
32. *loc. cit.*
33. Daniel Silverman, "Clinical and Electroencephalographical Studies on Criminal Psychopaths," *Archives of Neurology and Psychiatry,* I (July, 1943), pp. 18-20, 30-31.
34. George N. Thompson, *The Psychopathic Delinquent and Criminal* (Springfield: Charles C. Thomas, 1953).
35. Cressey *op. cit.,* p. 47.
36. *ibid.*, p. 48.
37. *loc. cit.*
38. One such attempt was made by David Abrahamson, *The Psychology of Crime* (New York: John Wiley & Sons, Inc., 1960).
39. John Dollard, *Frustration and Aggression* (New Haven: Yale University Press, 1939).
40. Alfred Lindesmith, *The Addict and the Law* (New York: Random House, Inc., 1965), p. 132. John Clausen, "Social and

Psychological Factors in Drug Addiction," *Law and Contemporary Problems,* XXII (Winter, 1957), pp. 35-51.

41. Vern L. Bullough, "Streetwalking: Theory and Practice," *Saturday Review,* IIL (September 4, 1965), pp. 52-54.

42. Harold Greenwald, *The Call Girl* (New York: Ballantine Books, 1958).

43. Marshal B. Clinard, *Sociology of Deviant Behavior* (New York: Rinehart & Company, Inc., 1957), pp. 126-128.

44. Sutherland and Cressey, *op. cit.,* pp. 81-82.

45. For an excellent account of the learned nature of prostitution, see Oscar Lewis, *La Vida* (New York: Vintage Books, 1966).

46. Don Martindale, *The Nature and Types of Sociological Theory* (Boston: Houghton Mifflin Company, 1960), pp. 475-476.

47. Albert K. Cohen, *Delinquent Boys: The Culture of the Gang* (Glencoe: The Free Press, 1955), and Walter B. Miller, "Lower-Class Culture as a Generating Milieu of Gang Delinquency," *Journal of Social Issues,* XIV, No. 3 (1958), pp. 5-19.

48. Richard A. Cloward and Lloyd E. Ohlin, *Delinquency and Opportunity* (Glencoe: The Free Press, 1960).

49. Again, this is a theoretical treatment of the problem. Many prisons make no further effort to diagnose or treat a prisoner. The same is often true of some parole and probation officers.

50. For a further investigation of this approach to criminal classification, see Edwin Schur, *Crimes Without Victims* (Englewood Cliffs: Prentice-Hall, Inc., 1965).

51. Narcotics addiction is not always caused by psychological inadequacy. Many addicts begin drug use due to social pressures exerted by peer groups. Treatment of such individuals would generally entail a sociological approach.

52. Frank Hartung, *Crime, Law and Society* (Detroit: Wayne State University Press, 1965), pp. 62-84.

53. Eric Berne, *A Layman's Guide to Psychiatry and Psycho-Analysis* (3rd ed.; New York: Simon and Schuster, 1968), p. 215.

54. *ibid.,* pp. 216-217.

55. Don C. Gibbons, *Changing the Lawbreaker: The Treatment of Delinquents and Criminals* (Englewood Cliffs: Prentice-Hall Inc., 1965).

56. Although Gibbons constructed separate typologies for adult and juvenile offenders, we shall be concerned here with the adult offenders.

57. Gibbons, *op. cit.* pp. 253-282.

58. Karl F. Schuessler, "Parole Predictions: Its History and Status," *Journal of Criminal Law, Criminology and Police Science,* VL (December, 1954), pp. 425-431.

59. Michigan Council on Crime and Delinquency, *The Saginaw Probation Demonstration Project* (Lansing, 1963), pp. 32-34.

60. University of California School of Criminology, *The San Francisco Project: A Study of Federal Probation and Parole,* Research Report No. 14, (Los Angeles: University of California, 1969), pp. 6-9.

61. Walter B. Miller, "The Impact of a 'Total Community' Delinquency Control Project," *Social Problems* X (Fall, 1962), pp. 176-186.

62. In an interview granted to William R. Lamoreaux, printed in "Exploding Some Myths," *Michigan Challenge*, IX (September, 1969), p. 13.
63. "Parole Board," *Life*, July 10, 1970, p. 57.
64. South Carolina Department of Corrections, *Project First Change* (Columbia, 1969).
65. John Conrad, *Crime and Its Correction* (Berkeley: University of California Press, 1965), pp. 82-83.
66. J. Edgar Hoover, *op. cit.*, p. 37.
67. *U. S. News & World Report*, March 16, *op. cit.*, p. 17.
68. A comparison of the "crime clock" charts in the F.B.I. Uniform Crime Reports of 1963 (p. 17), and 1969 (p. 29).
69. Alvin W. Cohn, "Contemporary Correctional Practice: Science or Art?" *Federal Probation*, XXXIV (September, 1970), p. 20.

VI. RESOCIALIZATION IN INDUSTRY: TRAINING FOR THE HARD-CORE UNEMPLOYED

A. NATURE AND EXTENT OF THE PROBLEM

1. The Hard-Core Unemployed

Resocialization in industry is most often considered to be training for the hard-core unemployed. It is important to distinguish, however, between those who are unemployed and those who are hard-core unemployed. In October, 1970, there were approximately 4.3 million Americans without jobs. Of that number, most were only temporarily unemployed and qualified to find work in the future. In California, for example, an estimated 20,000 to 30,000 engineers were out of work due to government cutbacks in defense and research spending. Nearly 25,000 textile workers in Georgia and the Carolinas were on lay-off. All in all, a total of 1,874,000 blue-collar workers and 1,213,000 white-collar workers in the United States were out of work in 1970.[1] The crucial difference between the unemployed and the hard-core unemployed is the *reason* for their unemployment. The unemployed are out of work due to the state of the economy. Should the economy become more vitalized, most of the unemployed would probably be called back to their former jobs or move to other positions. The hard-core unemployed, however, would probably remain without work regardless of the nature of the economy. The hard-core unemployed share a number of common social characteristics which, as investigation will reveal, preclude a normal working career without the aid of some form of resocialization.

A report prepared for the Manpower Administration

describes a cross section of the typical hard-core unemployed this way: They are usually functionally illiterate and their work habits are bad. They have been in school through the sixth grade, unemployed for 18 months, and have no personal transportation. Both they and their parents are unskilled; they live with one and one-half families. They can afford to eat only twice a day, have seen a physician only once in their lives, and now need eyeglasses and dental work. They are married and each has three children. Almost half are Negroes, one-fourth are Spanish-speaking, and three-fourths are male.[2] They usually live in areas with a relatively high degree of social pathology and many have accrued some sort of criminal record. Few can remember ever working steadily and, if so, rarely at a skilled job. They are often under 22 years of age or older than 45.

It is rather difficult to estimate how many Americans are hard-core unemployed. Considering that many poor people are often missed by census takers, and that the poor are often hard-core unemployed, any estimate must be considered tentative. Nevertheless, there seems to be general agreement that there are approximately one million hard-core unemployed in the U.S.[3] This is, however, a very conservative estimate and, depending on one's point of view, could be raised. According to the Interagency Manpower Planning Task Force, there are currently about 11 million persons chronically in poverty. For them, better employment is a possible solution to their own poverty and to the poverty of their dependents. About two-thirds of these people (7 million) possess inadequate education and training for the skills required in today's job market. About 1.5 million suffer from physical, mental, or emotional instability but could still be prepared for more productive work. The great majority of them are probably further handicapped by lack of knowledge of what kinds of jobs and training are available, where they are, and how to make application.[4]

As will become increasingly evident, the hard-core unemployed resemble the undereducated and the criminal recidivist in many ways. Socially, they tend to occupy the lower class levels. In terms of personal preparation, most are unable to cope with life outside of their relatively narrow scope of experiences. In essence, the under-educated, criminal recidivist, and hard-core unemployed are often one and the same person. For this reason, the development and treatment of their social problems are quite similar.

2. History and Scope of Training for the Hard-Core Unemployed

The history of aid to the unemployed should not be confused with the history of training for the hard-core unemployed. Either privately or publicly, the unemployed have been offered help since the founding of this country. In the early days of our nation, many were cared for under locally financed and administered poor laws. This situation was altered during the nineteenth century in that specialized treatment was given to specific groups of the poor and greater reliance was placed upon private charity to deal with poverty that was presumably due to unemployment. From about 1870 to well into the present century, most welfare authorities believed only a private charity could give relief in a way that would preserve the self-respect of the clients. It was not until the depression of the thirties that the state governments, and eventually the federal, realized that private charities were unable to cope with the problem without help.[5] By the nineteen-sixties, tremendous advances had been made in providing social and financial services to the unemployed. Systems of unemployment insurance were set up nationally after passage of the Social Security Act of 1935. In 1961, the program of Aid to Dependent Children was amended to include children of the unemployed. Other indications of concern for the unemployed have been the Employment Act of 1946, the Area Redevelopment Act of 1961, the Manpower Development and Training Act of 1962, and the Public Works Acceleration Act of 1962.[6]

Although the concern shown for the unemployed often benefited the hard-core unemployed, the hard-core unemployed have not been of special concern for very long. Recalling the efforts of Carver and DuBois to reeducate Negroes, we might consider that these and subsequent projects were training for the hard-core unemployed. It would be more accurate to state, however, that training programs specifically aimed at those whom we consider hard-core are, for the most part, less than two decades old.

During the fifties, a few private groups began responding to the needs of the hard-core unemployed. An example is the Trade Union Leadership Council (TULC), which was founded in Detroit in 1957 by union members and officials. Without federal assistance and mainly through local contributions and energy, the TULC provided a variety of training for over 550 Negroes within a two-year period.[7] Private industry has been involved, to varying degrees, with training of the hard-core unemployed for almost a decade. The McDonnell-Douglas Corporation in St. Louis, Missouri, has had training experience with the hard-core dating back to 1963. In its earlier efforts, the company trained about 3,000 individuals for relatively unskilled work and has trained smaller groups for clerical and in-plant food services.

For the past decade, state and federal governments have been concerned with the problems of the hard-core unemployed. Although some states have had fair employment laws for some time, the Federal Civil Rights Acts of 1957 and 1964 did a great deal to open opportunities to members of racial and ethnic minorities among whose ranks were thousands of hard-core unemployed. The civil disorders which began in 1965 and have continued since have also done a great deal to awaken the nation to the plight of the hard-core. Realizing that six out of seven jobs are in private industry, President Johnson, in 1968, called upon the National Alliance of Businessmen (NAB), headed by Henry Ford II, to join with the government in locating, hiring, and training the hard-core unemployed. Through a program entitled Job Opportunities in the Business Sector (JOBS), private industry first hires, then trains the hard-core with the help of Federal subsidies. The cost of training runs from $2,500 to $3,000 per individual, yet this cost, in some instances, is borne by industry alone.

Although there are numerous local programs, JOBS is by far the most extensive national attempt at meeting the needs of the hard-core unemployed. Nearly 25,000 firms participate in training programs and will be supported by an estimated $400 million to be allocated by the Labor Department. The NAB goal is to have 614,000 trainees hired and working by June, 1971. In September of 1969, the NAB counted 315,949 jobs already pledged by industry. More than 255,000 had been hired to fill those positions and 136,000 were still on the job.[8] A more recent estimate, reported in a July, 1970, issue of *U. S. News and World Report*, claimed that nearly 200,000 hard-core were working.[9]

B. THEORIES ON THE ETIOLOGY AND TREATMENT OF THE HARD-CORE UNEMPLOYED

1. Objective Factors

Many of the hard-core unemployed have become so, not due to personal inadequacy, but because of social pressures directed against them. The American Negro is, for example, overrepresented in the ranks of the hard-core unemployed.[10] The relationship between racial discrimination and subsequent occupational and social deprivation has been well documented and will not be repeated here.[11] Nonetheless, racial discrimination has manifested itself in such a way as to necessitate its inclusion in any discussion of the hard-core unemployed.

Due to sociological and psychological reasons, or as a result of group conflict, the dominant American society has consistently excluded Negroes from full participation in various spheres of institutional life. They have been denied entrance to many educational institutions and apprenticeship programs open to whites. As a result, the level of Negro education is below that of the white. Furthermore, the Negro is inferior in terms of vocational education, thus further reducing his ability to compete for jobs. Even where schooling and vocational opportunities are open to the Negro, these opportunities are often inferior to those offered whites. Since so many jobs in contemporary American society require considerable skills in mathematics or reading and writing, many Negroes, having been deprived of proper education, are unable to perform according to occupational requirements.

Even if a Negro manages to secure education and training equal to a white, he often faces discrimination in hiring and promotion. Many employers refuse to hire Negroes for responsible positions or, in many cases, for any position at all. Aware of this fact, many Negroes are reluctant even to seek work in the private sectors of industry. Those who do elect to seek out and find employment often find that working does nothing to advance them in life. Many jobs pay no more than minimum wages and, if at all possible, many employers will pay even less than that. Some jobs, such as dishwasher, errand boy, janitor, parking-lot attendant, and laborer pay less than $55 take-home pay for a five-day week. Considering the fact that welfare allotments in many states can support a man and his family almost as well (or better) than such a meager salary will allow, it is not surprising that many individuals choose not to work.

Discrimination is not confined to the Negro. Members of most minority groups, at one time or another, have been subjected to educational and job discrimination. Indians, Spanish-speaking Americans, southern Appalachians, and others have been excluded from opportunities in many sectors of life. Recalling the self-fulfilling prophecy, it becomes more obvious how those who discriminate are able to justify their actions. When education and opportunity are refused to any group, that group will contain a certain number of uneducated and inexperienced individuals. An employer can then deny jobs to members of this group and justify his actions by stating that they are either too lazy or incapable of performing the necessary work when, in fact, it was the dominant society, of which the employer is a part, which forced them into this position initially.

Other objective factors serve to keep many individuals in the ranks of the hard-core unemployed. Many jobs available to the hard-core are quite menial and demand a great deal of strength and stamina. Jobs in foundries and with construction companies usually call for an immense output of energy. The general poor health of the lower classes prohibits many of the hard-core unemployed from performing such demanding work. Where the nature of the work is no problem, many cannot pass the pre-employment physicals required by most major employers, thus further reducing employment opportunities. Even if their health is sufficient, the nature of menial work does little to inspire job loyalty. Liebow writes of one man's turmoil with his job: "Nancy tried to shake him awake. 'No more digging,' Richard cried out. 'No more digging! I can't do no more God-damn digging!' When Nancy finally managed to wake him, he dressed quickly and went to work. Richard stayed on the job two more weeks, then suddenly quit, ostensibly because his paycheck was three dollars less than he thought it should have been."[12]

Many of the hard-core unemployed cannot get jobs because of their backgrounds. Even if they are capable of performing the kind of work required for a job, their lack of work references discourages some employers from hiring them. Others have accrued some sort of police record and are considered poor security risks by potential employers and bonding agencies. Occasionally, hard-core unemployed will falsify an application regarding police records, only to be fired whenever the company double-checks the application.

Many potential jobs are located across town or in neighboring cities and require substantial travel to and from work for most employees. Most often, however, the hard-core do not own automobiles and cannot arrange a driving pool. Public transportation is often undependable, too time consuming or practically nonexistent. Thus, even if offered a job in a somewhat distant plant, there are many who could not accept due to lack of transportation.

To rectify the objective conditions which help keep individuals in the ranks of the hard-core unemployed, extensive social change is necessary. First and foremost, racial and cultural discrimination in education, vocational training, and employment must be eliminated. To do this, the Federal government will need to assume broader investigatory and proscriptive powers and apply these powers to all levels of public and private enterprise. Since it is virtually impossible for the government to control all phases of industrial activity, it is necessary to gain the consent and cooperation of industry itself. Propaganda campaigns, community education programs, and other means of persuasion should be employed in order to combat prejudice and discrimination.

The establishment of higher minimum wages and more effective control of economic inflation might serve to increase the purchasing power of individuals in the lower income brackets. Although minimum wage laws are generally passed to benefit the poor, these laws often come too late and provide too little. By the time a wage law takes effect, the economy has already moved so far ahead that any potential increase in purchasing power has been negated by inflation. Many welfare and provisional aid regulations serve to keep individuals on public relief rolls. Under most existing structures, individuals are financially penalized if they receive any income in addition to support payments. Some form of incentive program must be developed so that members of the hard-core find it more profitable to work than not to.

In order to help the hard-core unemployed perform their work, the government should provide whatever medical and dental care is needed in order to make them fit for jobs. The costs of these health programs could be borne by the government and repaid by the workers, or the costs could be shared by industry, government, and the individual. The nature of menial work might somehow be mitigated by job rotation, increased and varied work breaks, and other means. Continuing on-the-job training and an opportunity to advance to better work and higher pay would probably aid the worker in adjusting to the temporary circumstances of a menial job. Transportation difficulties could be overcome with a coordinated approach by industrial and public officials. A system of bus or train transportation designed specifically for heavy employers would probably be beneficial not only to the parties directly concerned but would serve to alleviate congestion in industrial areas. Employers should also be persuaded to place less emphasis on previous work histories and criminal records and instead measure the individual by his performance on the job alone.

The various objective factors which help keep many in the ranks of the hard-core unemployed eventually take their toll on the psyche of the individual. Chronic unemployment and its concurrent social consequences affect the cognitive processes in such a way that, even if offered a lucrative and satisfactory job, many hard-core unemployed would not be equal to the task. There are subjective socio-historical factors, generally stemming from the objective situation, which preclude normal employment without the aid of resocialization.

2. Subjective Factors

The hard-core unemployed view work in about the same emotional context as the culturally disadvantaged underachiever views school. Just as school is foreign and threatening to the underachiever, industry and the responsibility of a job often scare the hard-core unemployed. The hard-core unemployed have had a history of failures in industry. Due to objective and subjective reasons, most hard-core have an erratic work record punctuated by dismissals and lay-offs. The old adage, "last hired, first fired," is the story of their lives. In those instances where they were put on a job, they were given little or no responsibility and expected to work like machines rather than human beings. The hard-core unemployed have been manipulated, embarrassed, denied, and often brutalized in the world of industry. Not surprisingly, many view the taking of a job as the surrender of masculinity and total subjugation to a supervisor. . . all for $1.60 an hour!

The hard-core are also quite naive regarding the ways of

the factory and office. Family and neighborhood experiences tend to alienate them from the "world of work." They do not overhear relatives, neighbors, and friends in "shop talk" about incidents and aspirations relating to the job. No casual conversations and informal relations introduce them to the jargon, costumes, manners, and subtleties of office and shop. Nor do they acquire familiarity with office and factory tools by playing with daddy's briefcase or tool kit or by having daddy drive them to see his place of work.[13] Lower-class children are often denied contact with relevant work models. In their neighborhoods, most of the men are either without work, on aid, or sporadically employed. The children never internalize the fact that people rise early in the morning and go off to work five days a week. Those individuals in their neighborhood who acquire and keep steady employment often move away to secure better living conditions. Even those who work steadily and still remain in the neighborhood very seldom talk about their job experiences. Since the work of most members of the lower class is relatively dull and repetitious, there is little to discuss. Unlike many members of the middle class, lower-class workers leave their job both physically and mentally when quitting time arrives.

In reaction to the poor job opportunities available to them, many of the hard-core have developed the notion that work is for "squares." They believe that they would be foolish to take a job, that such an endeavor never leads to anything and is reserved for those who know no better. Other means of securing income appear more attractive. The pimp in his Cadillac and the numbers-runner with a bankroll offer a more favorable image to many of the hard-core unemployed then does the tired, menial laborer coming home from work with soot on his pants and just a few dollars in his pocket.

Many of the hard-core unemployed have never internalized a "work ethos." They cannot perceive the relationship between effort and advancement. For example, the hard-core seldom sees friends and relatives work their way up from janitors and maids to managerial workers or office staff. Hard work and extra effort may be a necessary condition of keeping a job but it seldom leads to promotion. Thus, the hard-core tend to question the value of initiative, extra effort, and self-improvement. Although lack of initiative on a job might appear to be mere laziness, it can also be viewed as pragmatic realism. The experiences of many hard-core unemployed have demonstrated that self-improvement and increased effort often tend to multiply and intensify frustrations and unhappiness. Rather than being rewarded with a promotion, they may be given more work.

In some instances, the hard-core either refuse or drop out of certain training programs which promise them a more secure future. Their reasons for dropping out are generally difficult for the middle-class person to accept yet, nonetheless, there is evidence of pragmatic realism. Most training programs require an extensive commitment of time and energy. The stipend, however, is generally scarcely enough to cover food and rent. Thus, enrollment in a program often involves an acceptance of a lengthy impoverishment for one's self and family and a considerable social confinement from many leisure-time activities.[14] Many of the hard-core do not believe it is worth the effort, particularly when they are not certain they will be hired upon the termination of training or, if hired, that they will be treated fairly.

The hard-core unemployed may fail to maintain employment due to a tendency to flee from tension-ridden situations. Fear of not succeeding on a job or of being unable to cope with ambivalence is not unusual in a person who lacks self-identity, ego strength, and a background reservoir of positive experiences. Many job situations continually threaten the sense of competence of the hard-core. Rather than stay on a job and face the possibility of being fired (the hard-core often believe it is a *probability*), it is easier to find some excuse to quit. This escape mechanism allows the maintenance of self-esteem. Thus, they can believe "If I had been able to keep the job, I know I would have succeeded."[15]

Some of the hard-core have simply "given up." At one

point in their lives, many seriously attempted to find work and possessed a positive mental attitude towards industry. For a variety of reasons (e.g. slow economy, prejudice, lack of skills, etc.), they were unable to gain employment, even after looking for months on end. If one considers the psychological factors involved in seeking work, the relationship between lack of success and despair becomes clear. When an individual asks an employer for work, he is placing himself, his family, and their futures at the employer's mercy. If the employer says, "yes," the job-seeker's entire life-style could change; if he says "no," he may be relegated to poverty. Thus, there is a lot at stake when a man asks another for a job. Many employers, however, handle the situation quite insensitively. A curt "no" can hurt a job-seeker's ego much more than expected. Considering the fact that many job-seekers are told "no" ten times a day for months or years on end, it is not surprising that they give up looking. Few men like to place themselves in a position to be hurt.

Federal and state employment agencies do little to rebuild a man's sense of pride. The atmosphere at most employment offices is cold and impersonal. At any given time, there are scores of men milling about, waiting to be called. Some are called but, for many job-seekers registered with employment offices, the wait is interminable, especially if they are unskilled. To many hard-core, government employment offices seem to be all paperwork and no jobs.

The personnel of certain manpower retraining programs have complained that the lack of essential socio-occupational skills among the hard-core often renders them untrainable as well as unemployable. When selected for training, many display high rates of absenteeism, tardiness, and a lack of classroom decorum. Psychologists have interpreted this behavior as either the result of insufficient information about appropriate dress, punctuality, etc., or as evidence of the subtle, almost ceaseless battle which many hard-core conduct against a society traditionally viewed as their enemy.

Many of the hard-core unemployed remain so due to a

lack of learning and test-passing skills. Despite their relatively adequate intellectual capacity, mastery of unfamiliar material, in view of the attendant frustrations and anxiety-producing factors, requires a supreme effort. They often view on-the-job training as they did learning in school—with fear or antagonism. Even when the hard-core attempt to master a vocational skill which requires home study, home conditions might prevent concentrated effort. Few have comfortable or separate places for study in their crowded homes, and noises in adjacent apartments and streets often distract them.[16] Furthermore, their neighborhood peers might discourage home study by continuing social demands by mocking the "school boy."

Liebow considers the orientation toward time held by the hard-core to be a result rather than a cause of their chronic unemployment. Many members of the lower classes have generally been considered unable to delay gratification. That is, they live in the present and do not plan for the future. Thus, an individual may squander a week's pay in two days or lose the entire amount in a "crap" game. Whereas some social scientists have explained this behavior as an inability to perceive and plan for the future, Liebow states that the hard-core live for the moment *because* of what they see in the future. The future of the hard-core is often no better than the past. The constant awareness of a future loaded with "trouble" results in a constant readiness to move, leave town, or seek pleasure immediately, while it is still possible. Constant feelings of insecurity discourage many hard-core unemployed from making deep and lasting commitments to friends, family and job. To make commitments is to limit freedom of movement and to many of the hard-core, freedom of movement is their one last security.[17]

Moynihan has explained chronic unemployment of Negro males in the context of a matriarchial family structure. In the over-all picture of the Negro subculture, women have held a more favorable economic position than men. Because many men cannot support their family, they either desert or remain continually subservient to their wives. A boy growing up with such a male model is usually unable to develop positive self-definitions or to later assume adequate roles demanded of adult males. This psychological state is generally transferred from one generation to the next, along with continued family instability, unemployment, and dependency upon public aid.[18]

Before the hard-core unemployed can be expected to develop and maintain adequate work habits, the subjective factors mentioned in previous pages must be dealt with. First, however, the objective situation must open up to permit equal access to training and occupational positions. Once this is done, the hard-core unemployed, and probably a subsequent generation, will need help in adjusting psychologically to their new opportunities in the industrial arena. The adjustment will be difficult at first and will require enlightenment and patience on the part of management and supervisory personnel. A better understanding of the attitudes of the hard-core might help their advisors and instructors. It is often assumed that the disadvantaged are unmotivated to work. In view of the poor quality of jobs generally available to them, motivation (or an apparent lack of it) may be more related to the quality of perceived opportunity than to anything intrinsic in the disadvantaged individual. Since motivation is related to attitudes, and since behavioral scientists believe that attitudes change after action changes and not before, "proper" attitudes will develop when the individual is involved in appropriate action.[19] In other words, if opportunity increases, attitudes toward work become more favorable.

Aside from having jobs opened to them, the hard-core will require a number of supporting services. Extensive orientation programs aimed at familiarizing them with job requirements will be necessary. In an effort to compensate for a lack of job-related experiences, extensive role-playing should be employed. Most of the hard-core will probably experience anxiety in the job situation. In order to settle their nerves and allay the fears developed over years of failure, counseling and therapy should be made available to the hard-core. They should also be given accelerated academic and vocational training to compensate for existing deficiencies. Since they tend to fear classrooms, or anything else related to the school setting, on-the-job instruction and in-plant training sessions would be most appropriate. Until their lack of reading and mathematical ability can be overcome, special visual devices should be used in the place of signs or computations. Deficiencies in school-related skills will hamper their performance on any kind of advancement test. Where progress needs to be measured, work samples rather than written scores should be the criteria. Since the hard-core have learning disabilities not common to regular job trainees, perhaps a low teacher-pupil ratio would be of critical importance.

It is important that the hard-core perceive a future which can be improved by their own efforts. They should not be trained for "nowhere" jobs or have job positions "created" for them. Jobs without substance are perceived as such by both the hard-core and industrial comptrollers as well. If vocational upgrading is going to have lasting effects, the hard-core must be trained to do work which is essential to primary, secondary, or tertiary economic activity. As soon as possible, trainees should be removed from their classes and given regular job status. The onus of being a "special hard-core trainee," although inescapable at first, might eventually serve to retard further advancement. Some trainees involved in exceedingly long projects may find the atmosphere so warm and pleasant as to prefer it to the real world. It also is possible that long-term trainees will tend to overemphasize their disabilities and suffer damage to self-esteem.[20]

Where necessary, substantial stipends should be allotted to those trainees who cannot afford to support their families during training. Although it is not customary, the hard-core must be paid almost as much while in training as they will be once the necessary skills are acquired. Only in this way will many of the hard-core be willing or able to commit themselves for any length of time to what they consider to be an uncertain venture. Social skills familiar to the middle class are often foreign to the disadvantaged. Instruction should be given in such areas as personal grooming and hygiene, money management, how to use various free public services, and how to use public transportation. Training is also necessary in person-to-person communication, listening, speaking, treatment of customers, and general business habits.

C. AN ANALYSIS OF TRAINING FOR THE HARD-CORE UNEMPLOYED

Although most training programs for the hard-core unemployed are similar in terms of theory and objectives, there are certain differences which bear investigation. One wide-spread program, Opportunities Industrialization Center, Inc., provides complete job training before allowing trainees to be hired by various employers. Founded by Dr. Leon Sullivan in Philadelphia, in 1964, OIC was originally a local project aimed at providing training for the city's 100,000 jobless Negroes. Because he did not have sufficient capital, Sullivan solicited aid from private parties and the municipal government. A Philadelphia philanthropist donated a six-story building and the city offered use of an abandoned, rat-infested jail. Unused or unwanted equipment such as tools, electronics gear, and a computer were also offered to OIC. The trainees presently learn such things as keypunch operation, industrial maintenance, and general retail work. The trainees are also given instruction in reading, writing, and mathematics, but it is called communication and computation so they will not be ashamed. Philadelphia businessmen were originally skeptical of OIC and were quite reluctant to hire graduates of its various training programs. Eventually, however, these same employers began asking for OIC workers.

OIC has greatly expanded its operations and now has 90 centers with 35,000 people in training throughout the country. The funding of these centers amounted to $23 million in 1969, with a substantial portion of this coming from the Office of Economic Opportunity and the Departments of Labor and Health, Education, and Welfare.[21]

The directors of OIC and government officials consider

the program to be an overwhelming success. They state that over 20,000 men and women, generally untrained and mostly black, went through OIC training and now hold jobs in a wide range of skills. They have added $40 million in new income to the national economy and have reduced by $10 million the annual cost of welfare and other assistance to cities, states, and the federal government. [22]

The National Alliance of Businessmen operates a job-training program entitled Job Opportunities in the Business Sector (JOBS). This program persuades employers to hire the hard-core *first* and then give them needed training. Any expense beyond normal training requirements is underwritten by the federal government. Using personnel loaned by private industry, JOBS approaches potential employers and asks them to consider hiring and training those individuals who have been certified as disadvantaged by the appropriate state agency. In general, the training period may last from 8 to 45 weeks, depending on the skill level of the occupation. Under the "hire first" principle, the disadvantaged worker is paid usual wages for the entry-level position. The worker is given all benefits provided to, and is subject to, the same rules and regulations as other employees. The trainees are also given extensive on-the-job training, classroom work, and provided with a counseling service. The employer may provide these services with company personnel or it may subcontract this responsibility.

JOBS also offers a job-upgrading contract available to employers who have previously held JOBS contracts or who are about to be awarded one. The idea is to provide additional training and supportive services to persons already employed in order to move them to jobs at higher skill levels. The Department of Labor reimburses the employer for the extraordinary costs of training based on the starting hourly wage rates and the number of hours of training required for the occupation. This also covers the cost of instruction, nonproductive time, extra wastage, added wear and tear of equipment, and added supervisory effort. The NAB advertises a high rate of success for its program and hopes to expand. [23]

The Chase Manhattan Bank operates a six-week training program aimed at teaching hard-core youth skills associated with banking. Bank officials believe a weekly paycheck helps to motivate the trainees. They are paid $1.60 an hour during the course and are paid $75.00 a week once they come on the payroll. They are given entry-level positions such as keypunch operator, sorting and listing clerk, and stock clerk. After beginning actual work, the trainees are required to spend about ten hours each week getting further instruction in reading, math, and language. The program provides six teachers for each class of twenty youths. All are specialists in remedial teaching and many have taught in underdeveloped areas. Program officials claim that such intensive instruction can raise the academic level of trainees an average of two years in six weeks. The trainees are motivated by promises of promotion and financial gain in return for dedication and hard work. The bank pays for the training itself, an average of $1,000 a student. Officials believe the program is an outstanding success and state that 80% of the trainees who started in the program in December, 1967, were still working by August, 1968. The bank intends to expand its training programs and hopes to train about 1,000 hard-core unemployed within a three-year period.[24]

Most training schedules make provisions for some form of orientation and counseling for hard-core trainees. Although the value of these services seems quite widely accepted, there has been evidence that neither orientation programs nor therapeutic counseling groups do anything to help the hard-core maintain employment. Rosen studied the effects of an on-the-job orientation program conducted at a large utility company for 170 new employees. The subjects were not defined as hard-core but their social circumstances implied a high probability that they would become so. To effectively test the impact of orientation on both employees and line supervisors, control and experimental groups were organized. An absolute control condition was provided by having neither supervisor nor employee given orientation. Under another condition both were given orientation. A third condition provided no orientation for supervisors but orientation for the new employees.

Orientation consisted of Role Playing Group Problem Solving (RPGPS) sessions. Supervisors were exposed to six two-hour sessions every other week for twelve weeks, in groups no larger than six supervisors. Employees were exposed to nine two-hour sessions. RPGPS orientation consisted of an initial playing out of problems by two members of the group. This was followed by a group critique and discussion, and finally by replaying the problem with the initial participants reversing roles. Sessions were conducted by Ph.D.'s in psychology who had had experience with both group techniques and Negroes of a lower socio-economic level. To determine whether the experimental groups had greater success integrating into the company structure, data were collected on turnover, absenteeism and, where feasible, merit rating.

The results of the study indicated no relationship between orientation and job stability. For the employees as a whole, whether or not they received orientation had no impact on turnover. The author of the study concluded that "such intervention had no impact and that one should seriously consider the high costs, in terms of time and effort involved for no apparent gain, before utilizing such methods in the future."[25]

In an earlier study conducted by the same researcher, 49 hard-core unemployed Negroes were hired by a large company and divided into two comparable groups. One group was given quasi-therapeutic treatment in the form of group counseling sessions. The therapist was university-affiliated and operated from an eclectic position, strongly influenced by both client-centered and modified psycho-analytic techniques involving empathy, clarification of feelings, interpretation of resistances, and analysis of transference feelings. The group received a total of 14 training sessions of one and one-half hours each, stretched over a 12-week period. The main thrust of each meeting was supposedly to discuss and resolve work-related problems.

The 25 men assigned to the company orientation program met as a unit and spent equivalent hours on the same schedule as did men in the therapy groups. Technically, they were to experience a passive audience role. They were exposed to lectures about the business, the customers served, history of the company, etc., and given tours of the plant's facilities. Although it was not part of the initial research design, employees in this group also partook in several question and answer sessions.

After ten weeks, supervisors of the two groups were asked whether or not they would recommend their hard-core subordinates for an increment. A greater percentage of the company-trained hard-core were recommended than those who had been exposed to therapeutic orientation. After six months, turnover and absenteeism data were evaluated. The company group had lower turnover rates than did the therapy group.

Analysis of the university-run orientation sessions indicated that men rejected talking about work problems and preferred to spend their time exhibiting hostility toward white institutions in general. From the company point of view, all levels except high management moved from positive attitudes toward the program to one of neutrality about continuing such programs in the future. It was also clear that other workers reacted negatively to the more lenient standards of selection and/or discipline accorded the hard-core unemployed.[26]

There are indications that, at least in some programs, there is widespread apathy among supervisors and trainees alike. Rutledge and Gass published a study of the careers of nineteen Negro males engaged in a 52-week training program in practical nursing. Although the authors did not make any specific statements regarding the social atmosphere of the training program, their chapter on "Results and Recommendations" seemed to imply that attitudes were abrasive at times.[27] The authors also made comments about earlier programs designed to train hard-core males. For example, they stated that "Previous attempts to train the disadvantaged Negro man for service occupation had met with high spontaneous drop-out and ultimate failure rates or poor work records for many of those who did not complete the prescribed training."[28]

There appears to be mounting criticism of training programs for the hard-core unemployed. The *U. S. News and World Report* magazine surveyed training programs across the nation in July of 1970, and arrived at the following conclusion: "A costly federal effort to turn unskilled poor people into wage earners is falling short of its goals. On-the-scene reports show more than the economic slump is to blame."[29] A subcommittee report of the Senate Labor Committee found the national JOBS program has been badly managed and oversold as the answer to the troubles of the hard-core unemployed. Although Detroit seems to be making headway with the program, Atlanta reports high dropout rates and little success in placing trainees. Programs to train the hard-core unemployed in the Los Angeles area are so myriad and overlapping that no one knows if they are at all effective. The vice chairman of the Los Angeles Human Relations Commission says: "These so-called noble experiments aren't really training programs. They are WPA-type projects." Yet Chicago reports a retention rate of 54.8 percent and officials in that city believe that, with a few modifications, they can achieve higher rates. In Houston, according to critics in the U. S. Department of Labor, efforts to train and find jobs for the unemployed are inconclusive and the program has been mismanaged. [30]

Some authorities have criticized certain basic theories on which many programs operate. One knowledgeable public official has stated that the relatively brief training periods are totally incapable of reversing a lifelong involvement in the cycle of failure and adjustment to failure. He also believes that businessmen have over-estimated worker initiative and have assumed that a disillusioned low-skilled worker has the same basic drive as a middle-class worker. In order to reduce the dropout rate, which is close to 50% for most programs, companies should not be so lenient with ghetto trainees. Realistic standards for work habits and programs in learning must be set and firmly maintained.[31]

Equitable Life Assurance Society of the U. S. has had experience with hard-core training programs dating back to 1962. In their first training program, 22 high school dropouts had to be hired to fill eight jobs, owing to high "quit" rates. Of these, 14 worked less than one year, six performed in a satisfactory way for up to three years. None was with Equitable by 1968. A second training program was altered somewhat but results were the same. In a third plan, Equitable brought girls into the program, mostly for typing jobs. For the mixed group, the results were: 6 of 24 boys and 8 of 15 girls performed satisfactorily for from one year to three. Yet, eighteen of the boys and seven of the girls worked less than a year. Eight boys and two girls were fired for poor performance. A fourth plan had similar results. All in all, only 24 out of 122 trainees made the grade and moved up the ladder with promotions. Reasons for leaving varied from lack of satisfaction with the job to excessive absenteeism and tardiness.[32]

In an evaluation of government-backed training for the hard-core unemployed, Gerald Somers wrote that "government-subsidized retraining has thus far achieved only minor reductions in unemployment." His reasons for this failure relate to the limited period of experience with retraining the hard-core, the state of the economy, and the scale of the programs relative to the number of unemployed.[33] Whereas Somers places the blame for failure on objective conditions, Dizard looks to the attitudes of many Negroes for an explanation. Rather than accept his traditional subordination in work contexts, the Negro can work his way out of demeaning circumstances by playing the "system" for what it is worth—to "hustle." Reports from various instructors in training programs indicate that many trainees refer to their internship as the "poverty hustle." This indicates that their interest is hardly one of getting into the occupational structure. Instead of working to join the system, they are working to beat it.[34]

Various other aspects of training for the hard-core unemployed have been criticized. It has often been argued that those hired into programs are not the "true" hard-core but represent the "cream of the crop." The real hard-core unemployed are usually turned away due to poor health, excessive criminal records, possible narcotics addiction, or poor attitudes. Thus, only those who represent the employers' idea of the hard-core are hired, and these are usually men in more favorable circumstances. Relatively arbitrary guidelines are often used to "certify" an individual as disadvantaged and thus eligible for entry into a training program. For example, to be eligible for government-sponsored training programs in Detroit, an applicant must live within the confines of a meandering street called Grand Boulevard. Officials in Washington, who originally designated these boundaries, seem unaware of the fact that a great number of hard-core unemployed live in other areas of the city and, *ipso facto*, are not qualified. Another criticism is the unrealistic wage guidelines applied to training program applicants. If an individual earns more than $1,800 in the previous year, he is not considered "disadvantaged" and thus is ineligible for training. It appears that an individual earning $1,900 would be considered "too well off" or not in need of job training and placement. Such an unrealistic and relatively arbitrary wage limitation defeats the purpose of the entire program, especially when certain individuals may have numerous dependents (although the ceiling is raised $600 for each) or be in any variety of financial difficulties.

Most job-training programs are funded by so many diverse agencies, subcontracted to so many different offices and run by such divergent personnel that very few people really know who does what. Program employees are usually fairly well educated, yet they still have trouble following a vague and often unknown procedure. In view of this, the entire situation must appear even more frightening to hard-core individuals trying to understand what it is they are going through. Even where a researcher is successful in learning where a potential source of information is, he will usually have difficulty getting anything but the most trivial information about training programs. The Chrysler Institute in Detroit, which handles Manpower programs, will not release to the general public any details concerning the failure or success of their efforts.[35]

There is no apparent explanation for the contradictory reports of many training programs for the hard-core unemployed. Whereas some projects report success, others report failure. Investigations of the theories and approaches utilized by these programs seldom reveal any significant differences. The staff and the applicants are quite similar in the training programs, so this does not explain the variance. It appears that further analysis will be necessary before this form of resocialization can be realistically assessed.

FOOTNOTES

1. "Who Are the Unemployed: Grass Roots Survey?" *U. S. News and World Report*, November 16, 1970, p. 55.
2. Russel K. Peterson and Bryson B. Rash, "Industry Learns to Train the Hardcore," *Education Digest*, XXXV (October, 1969), p. 35.
3. "In a Time of Layoffs, Trouble for the 'Hardcore'," *U. S. News and World Report*, July 13, 1970, p. 24.
4. Stanley H. Ruttenberg, "Manpower Training—The Seeds of a Dilemma," *Manpower*, I (January, 1969), p. 3.
5. Frank R. Breul, "Early History of Aid to the Unemployed in the United States," in *In Aid of the Unemployed*, ed. by Joseph M. Becker (Baltimore: The John Hopkins Press, 1965), p. 6.
6. *ibid.*, p. 7.
7. Albert A. Blum and Charles T. Schmidt, "Job Training Through Adult Education: A Second Chance for the Negro and the Community," in *Employment, Race and Poverty*, ed. by Arthur M. Ross and Herbert Hill (New York: Harcourt, Brace and World, Inc., 1967), p. 466.
8. "Hard-core Program Will Widen Its Base," *Business Week*, November 15, 1969, pp. 41-42.
9. *U. S. News & World Report*, July 13, 1970, *op. cit.*, p. 24.
10. In a foreword by A. Philip Randolph, p. v, of Louis A. Ferman, Joyce L. Kornbluh, and J. A. Miller, eds., *Negroes and Jobs* (Ann Arbor: The University of Michigan Press, 1968).
11. See Gunnar Myrdal, *An American Dilemma* (2 vols.; New York: McGraw-Hill Book Company, 1962).
12. Elliot Liebow, *Tally's Corner* (Boston: Little, Brown and Company, 1967), p. 50.
13. Joseph S. Himes, "Some Work-Related Cultural Deprivations of Lower-Class Negro Youths," Ferman, Kornbluh, and Miller, *op. cit.*, p. 189.
14. Aaron L. Rutledge and Gertrude Zeman Gass, *Nineteen Negro Men* (San Francisco: Jossey-Bass, Inc., 1967), pp. 36-7.

15. *ibid.*, pp. 25-27.
16. The hard-core unemployed generally live in the most disorganized areas of a city.
17. Liebow, *op. cit.*, pp. 64-71.
18. Ferman, Kornbluh, and Miller, *op. cit.*, pp. 402-404.
19. Judah Drob and Vernon Sheblak, "Training the Hard-Core Unemployed," *Manpower*, I (January, 1969), p. 29.
20. *ibid.*, p. 30.
21. "Opening Doors to Opportunity," *Nation's Business*, April, 1970, p. 52.
22. *ibid.*, p. 48.
23. Manpower Administration, U. S. Department of Labor, *Introducing Jobs '70*, pamphlet (Washington, D. C.: U. S. Government Printing Office, 1970).
24. "Training the 'Hard-Core'—A Top Banker Tells His Story," *U. S. News and World Report*, August 7, 1968, p. 53.
25. Hjalmar Rosen, *On-the-Job Orientation of Unemployed Skill Center Trainees and Their Supervisors*, unpublished research project sponsored by the U. S. Department of Labor, June 1, 1970, p. 7.
26. Hjalmar Rosen, *A Group Orientation Approach for Facilitating the Work Adjustment of the Hard-Core Unemployed*, unpublished research project sponsored by the U. S. Department of Labor, April 15, 1969, pp. 2-3.
27. Rutledge and Gass, *op. cit.*, pp. 34, 95, 106.
28. *ibid.*, pp. 6-7.
29. *U. S. News and World Report*, July 13, *op. cit.* p. 24.
30. *ibid.*, p. 26.
31. "Employing Ghetto Workers: Nine Lessons of Experience," *Management Thinking*, July, 1968, pp. 5-6.
32. "Employing the Employables: What Companies are Finding," *U. S. News and World Report*, August 12, 1968, *op. cit.*, p. 50.
33. Gerald G. Somers, "Training the Unemployed," in Joseph M. Becker, *op. cit.*, pp. 232-3.
34. Jan E. Dizard, "Why Should Negroes Work?" in Ferman, Kornbluh, and Miller, *op. cit.*, p. 407.
35. Or so the authors were told in a personal communication with a Chrysler official.

VII. COMMENTS ON THE USE OF COUNSELING AND PSYCHOTHERAPY IN RESOCIALIZATION

A. THE NATURE AND EXTENT OF COUNSELING AND PSYCHOTHERAPY

1. Definitions of Counseling and Psychotherapy

Most resocialization programs provide some form of psychologically supportive service to program participants. Depending on the particular institution involved and the perceived needs of the participants, supportive services can range from individual or group counseling to more intensive treatment, such as psychotherapy. In any case, it is generally believed that most individuals in need of resocialization require help in interpreting and accepting the goals of behavior intervention.

Ohlsen describes counseling as an accepting, trusting, and safe relationship between a counselor and one or more clients. Within this relationship, clients are helped to express and deal with disturbing feelings and thoughts. Through examination of motives and attitudes, they develop the courage and self-confidence to apply what they have learned in changing their behavior. Should their new behavior fail to work, they feel sufficiently secure within the counseling relationship to determine why. Some clients require further assistance to convey their new selves to peers and to help significant others understand and accept their new selves.[1]

Group counseling, on the other hand, is not merely individual counseling applied to groups. It is a planned process which includes, among other things, identification with, analysis by, and support from the group. It is a group method designed to help individuals with the normal emotional problems of everyday living as well as severe or serious problems. Group counseling involves permissiveness, protection, privileged communication, and changes in personality and behavior that take place more rapidly than in life in general.[2] In group counseling, individuals explore and analyze their problems together, serving a therapeutic purpose for one another. The objectives are to achieve increased maturity in terms of integration, acceptance of reality, adaptability, and responsibility for self. It is directed toward helping clients gain release from frustration, anxiety, and guilt so they may attain objective acceptance of their thoughts, feelings, and impulses.[3]

Individual and group counseling can be used interchangeably in most resocialization programs. The latter form of counseling is gaining increased acceptance not only due to its economy but owing to the fact that it produces results which the traditional form of individual counseling is sometimes unable to do. Certain clients react better in a group setting and become more involved in the counseling experience once they develop group ties. On the other hand, there are those who prefer the privacy of a one-to-one therapeutic relationship and who, if placed in a group situation, would find themselves unable to participate successfully.

Psychotherapy consists of those methods which depend on a direct interaction between patient and therapist. Operating on the learning process, psychotherapy attempts to bring about a process of growth in the patient. This change, however, is not an intellectual process. Psychotherapy does not take place primarily in the sphere of the intellect. Its basic principle is to re-expose the individual, through the use of symbols and under more favorable circumstances, to emotional situations he was unable to handle in the past. The goal of this treatment is to undergo a "corrective emotional experience." Since neuroses are generally the result of the repression of fears or traumas, the patient is usually unable or unwilling to trace the source of his ailment. Given the secure nature of the therapeutic situation, however, the patient dares reappraise his anxieties. Under ideal conditions, he finds that the emotional "danger" can be tolerated without resort to crippling defense mechanisms. When one conceives of psychotherapy as a relearning process, it is evident that the patient needs strong continuing motivation to work at his problems and that his relationship with the therapist is an evolving, integral part of the whole experience.[4]

Therapists may use a variety of approaches to psychotherapy. Although there is an emerging interest in group psychotherapy and related techniques, space limits this discussion to the more common practice of psychotherapy on a one-to-one basis. Client-centered therapy relies on the client to take the lead in the therapeutic process. The therapist does not intervene by asking questions or giving information and advice. His goal is to help the client develop in his own directions, and his intervention is limited to removing emotional obstacles which lie in the client's path. The one therapeutic tool used in client-centered therapy is the acceptance, recognition, and clarification of feeling. The therapist restates whatever the client says, but he restates the affective nature of the comments rather than the content. The therapist learns to perceive things as the client perceives them, to enter as fully as possible into the client's "internal frame of reference." Once the client becomes more aware of his own feelings, he develops an ability to make effective appraisals and experiences a decreasing need for the therapist.

A highly individualized form of psychotherapy is psychoanalysis. Although psychoanalysis is often adapted to the needs of both the therapist and patient, most forms have similar characteristics. Free association is a technique which calls for the verbalization of random thoughts. The patient is instructed to report everything that occurs to him. He is asked to assume a passive attitude and to eliminate all conscious control over his mental processes. The therapist actively interprets the thoughts of the client. This interpretation is not used to instruct the patient but to bring about a new feeling on his part. Standard psychoanalysis also makes extensive use of the transference neurosis. As treatment proceeds, the patient begins to manifest a variety of feelings toward the therapist. The patient's feelings regarding the analyst become highly intensified and are often related to unresolved sexual and emotional conflicts. The analysis of dreams also plays a vital part in psychoanalysis. Dreams are regarded as spontaneous free associations. They are used as starting points for further free associations and as objects of interpretation.

Client-centered therapy and psychoanalysis are both extreme forms of psychotherapy. The client-centered method is often criticized as too superficial. Psychoanalysis, on the other hand, if often considered to be too lengthy and more involved than necessary. A hybrid and increasingly popular approach called "psychoanalytically-oriented psychotherapy" seems to combine aspects of client-centered therapy and psychoanalysis. In this form of psychotherapy, the therapist is familiar with psychoanalytic principles. He acknowledges the importance of unconscious motivation, the defense mechanisms, sexual drives, and Freud's stages of psychosexual development. The therapist attempts to use these insights in understanding his patients and planning their treatment. Treatment is not carried out according to standard psychoanalytic technique, however, since there are usually considerable departures dictated by time limitations and other circumstances.[5]

2. The Scope of Counseling and Psychotherapy

Counseling is a very big enterprise in the United States. Almost all elementary and secondary school systems make some allowance for the counseling needs of their students. In order to train counselors for school positions, many universities offer two year counseling and/or social work degree programs on the graduate level. College students themselves are usually offered guidance through university-operated mental health clinics. Counseling is not restricted to the academic arena, however. Numerous corporations employ counselors in their personnel departments and encourage employees to utilize their services. Many baccalaureate holders are placed in positions where, although not specifically trained for the task, they are expected to act as counselors. Public housing employees, probation and parole officers, court workers, school-teachers, ministers, and even policemen are often cast in the role of counselor. Thus, it is difficult to estimate the exact extent of the counseling phenomenon.

The extent of psychotherapy, on the other hand, is somewhat easier to measure. This is because most states have licensing laws which control access to and practice of the profession. Generally, psychotherapy is practiced either by a clinical psychologist or by a psychiatrist.

A popular interest among professional psychologists is clinical psychology. The typical clinical psychologist works in an agency giving care of treatment, e.g., prison, hospital, juvenile court, etc. He may also practice privately or with other professional colleagues. Clinical psychologists who have a Ph.D. degree and undergo a period of internship qualify for a diploma in Clinical Psychology awarded by the American Board of Examiners in Professional Psychology, a body created by psychologists to certify the competence of psychologists working at high levels of professional responsibility. Those workers who deal more with vocational and educational guidance or minor difficulties in social adjustment think of themselves as counseling psychologists rather than clinical psychologists. They, too, are provided with a diploma from the American Board of Examiners in Professional Psychology. Not all psychologists are concerned with therapy and counseling, however. Of those psychologists surveyed by the National Science Foundation, nineteen percent were in clinical practice and six percent were in counseling practice.[6]

The U. S. government foresees a very rapid expansion of the psychological profession through the 1970's. A large increase is anticipated in the number of psychologists employed by state and local agencies as well as verterans' hospitals. In 1968, starting salaries for male psychologists having a master's degree averaged about $9,800. The median salary for those holding a Ph.D. was $14,500. The annual average salary for professors ranged from $9,700 for assistant professors to $16,000 for full professors. In certain branches of the federal government, those holding the doctoral degree averaged about $16,300 in 1968. [7] Psychotherapy is also practiced by psychiatrists who, in addition to holding an M.D. degree, spend a one to four year period in a psychiatric setting, usually a hospital. Training to reach the highest rung on the psychiatric ladder takes ten years after graduation from college. The future psychiatrist must undergo three years of medical school and one or two years of hospital internship, three years of psychiatric residency, and one year of practice as a private or institutional psychiatrist. Only at the end of this training is the practitioner eligible to take the examination given by the American Board of Psychiatry and Neurology. As of March, 1967, only 7,481 "diplomates" in psychiatry had been certified by the board.[8]

All psychiatrists are not diplomates. In the United States today, an estimated 20,000 psychiatrists are practicing privately or in mental hospitals, in teaching, or in research. Three thousand more are working under supervision and residency following graduation from medical school. It appears, however, that there is a considerable gap between the total of 23,000 available psychiatrists and the number actually needed. Ten thousand additional psychiatrists are said to be needed to fill existing and projected positions in mental hospitals, general hospitals, clinics, and community health programs. Whereas only two million Americans are receiving psychiatric treatment, it has been estimated that as many as 20 million have mild to severe psychiatric problems.

Psychiatry is a remunerative profession. Most hospital psychiatrists earn an average of $18,000 a year. Private psychiatrists in metropolitan areas charge between $30-$50 for an hour's session with a patient. Although some psychiatrists donate portions of their time to charitable or civic activities, the annual earnings of many private practitioners exceed $40,000.[9]

B. COUNSELING AND PSYCHOTHERAPY IN RESOCIALIZATION

1. Compensatory Education

Compensatory education programs make use of counselors at virtually all levels. Counselors serve in both an advisory and informative capacity in elementary school programs and are often called upon to interpret the activities of the school to the community. They are useful in aiding elementary school teachers in their adjustment to compensatory education programs and often serve as a "buffer zone" during periods of transition. In the advanced grades and in college, many culturally deprived youngsters rely on the services of counselors to adjust to the new academic milieu. Students are encouraged to take their academic and personal problems to counselors, who are considered to have the necessary expertise in facilitating social adjustment. It seems to be generally accepted that counseling services are important for the mental hygiene of all students and particularly for culturally deprived students involved in compensatory education.

Although psychotherapy is not usually a regular service offered by the educational institution, psychologists and psychiatrists are often employed or consulted by boards of education. School and clinical psychologists are called in to diagnose and refer problem children for appropriate treatment. In some cases, treatment is given by school psychologists themselves. Psychiatrists are often consulted before any major educational plans are finalized and, during times of institutional crisis, their advice is sometimes sought. Although psychotherapy is not sponsored by schools themselves, students often undergo treatment for school-related problems such as truancy, insubordination, and for certain learning difficulties. Compensatory education programs are seldom planned without including, at least in a consulting role, school and clinical psychologists and psychiatrists. Thus, in a very real way, counseling and psychotherapy are a vital and integral part of the educational institution.

2. Criminal Rehabilitation

Counseling is an important part of criminal rehabilitation. Each and every individual under control of correctional systems is assigned to a parole or probation officer or caseworker. Whether in a prison, half-way house, or free in the community, clients are expected to avail themselves of the counseling services provided by their supervisors. Although corrections workers are obligated to protect the state from hopelessly antisocial individuals, they are also expected to serve the client's emotional needs.

Since the avowed purpose of the correctional system is resocialization rather than retaliation, each man is exposed to supportive and corrective counseling for the duration of his association with the system. Incipient juvenile delinquents are often referred to social work agencies. Should the efforts of an agency prove fruitless and the juvenile becomes involved in further trouble, he is placed either in juvenile detention or under the care of juvenile caseworkers. If his criminality extends into adult life, he will probably be exposed to probation officers, prison caseworkers, and parole officers, in that order.

The services of clinical psychologists and psychiatrists are required daily by the criminolegal systems. Before sentencing a convicted felon, magistrates generally ask for a presentence investigation. Subjects are often referred to court psychiatric clinics where psychologists and psychiatrists make appropriate diagnoses and pass their recommendations on to the judges. Many individuals are placed on probation only on the condition that they seek continuous and extensive psychiatric care. Others are committed to hospitals for the criminally insane where they are supposed to be given psychotherapy. If they are considered sane and committed to confinement in a penitentiary, psychotherapy is often made available to them. Similar psychological services are provided for juveniles, but such care is often more extensive.

3. Training for the Hard-Core Unemployed

Training programs for the hard-core unemployed make

extensive use of counselors. Generally, every trainee is assigned a counselor and expected to discuss personal and work-related problems with him. Since most social scientists believe the transition from chronic unemployment and job irresponsibility to full and responsible employment can be quite difficult, supportive counseling services are deemed necessary. Not only do counselors aid trainees in personal adjustments, social adjustments are usually required. Many foremen and other training personnel are unaccustomed to working with the hard-core unemployed and require appropriate orientation concerning the backgrounds and psyches of the culturally and economically deprived.

Psychologists and psychiatrists, in addition to playing their frequent role as consultants in training programs, are often called upon to conduct group therapy sessions aimed at facilitating trainee integration into the working force. In smaller, more intensive training programs, trainees are usually given psychotherapeutic attention by project directors, who are often psychologists, or by professionals hired on a contingency basis. In many ways, counselors and psychotherapists have much the same duties and problems in industrial training programs as they do in compensatory education projects. Just as counselors and therapists are considered indispensable to compensatory education and criminal rehabilitation, they have become vital in resocialization programs aimed at training the hard-core unemployed.

C. AN ANALYSIS OF COUNSELING AND PSYCHOTHERAPY

Although the use of counseling and psychotherapy in resocialization seems to be widely accepted, there have been serious questions raised as to the efficacy of both. Before investigating these criticisms, it is necessary to discuss the difference between counseling and psychotherapy. Counseling has been defined as a therapeutic experience for individuals who do not have serious emotional problems. Thus, treatment is of shorter duration and more superficial. Psychotherapy, on the other hand, can be considered a therapeutic experience for emotionally disturbed individuals with more severe psychopathology. Such treatment becomes more extensive and searching. These things considered, psychotherapy differs from counseling primarily in terms of the persons (and problems) treated rather than the treatment process. Although some writers deplore this separation of counseling and psychotherapy, the following analysis will deal with the two as relatively distinct entities.

Although there is relative agreement on the personal characteristics of the "ideal" counselor, there appear to be no effective criteria for selecting and screening counselor-applicants. A review of the literature indicates that counselor educators can predict academic success in professional education better than counseling success. Another problem is the use of data collected during professional preparation. It is not sufficient to know how counselors perform in a practicum setting arranged by their teachers. The real test can only come when they are left to establish their own role in an actual counseling setting.[10]

A number of independent studies have questioned whether counseling intervention can produce desired behavioral consequences. One study investigated the effects of group counseling on college freshmen enrolled in teacher education. One group was counseled once a week and the other twice a week. When compared with controls, neither experimental group improved significantly on self-acceptance, the dogmatism scale, or preference for complexity. Another study identified 121 underachievers in 22 classrooms. The pupils were randomly assigned into five groups: group counseling, individual counseling, remedial reading, Hawthorne effect (see Chapter VIII, Section B), and a control group. The counseled groups were given 14 half-hour sessions by a total of six male counselors. None of the treatments resulted in significant improvement, either in grades or personality test scores.[11]

In a comprehensive review of approximately 100 studies on the efficacy of counseling, Gazda and Larsen found only about fifty percent of the studies reporting positive change. The criteria included improved grades, self-acceptance, better school behavior and attendance, and improved peer-group relations. Those studies which reported improvement, however, were often based on general descriptions. Inadequate use was made of operational terms and carefully controlled observation.[12] All in all, many studies of the counseling process are poorly designed and difficult to repeat. Although counseling has its critics, opposition seems minimal when compared to the mounting attacks on psychotherapy in general and psychoanalysis in particular.

Andrew Salter begins his attack on psychoanalysis by noting the number of conflicting schools and persuasions within the whole area of psychoanalytic therapy. Considering the disagreement over theories and approaches by so many professionals, how can a layman know whether or not he is receiving valid treatment? Psychoanalysis, based on the writings and philosophy of Sigmund Freud, is, according to Salter, completely nonscientific and intuitive. Not only does Salter take psychoanalysts to task for their failure to employ the scientific method, or even to re-evaluate theory in the light of feedback, but he also attributes psychic degeneration to the process itself. One analyst was asked what would happen if a normal person were to undergo psychoanalysis. He replied, "Even though he were normal at the beginning of the analysis, the analytic procedure would create a neurosis."[13]

Salter believes that the analyst "sprinkles and buries false nuggets of Oedipus, castration (or penis envy), and bisexuality." Then, when the patient digs where he is directed to dig and uncovers certain ideas placed in his mind by the analyst, both the analyst and analysand feel the treatment is coming along well.[14] Psychoanalysis rests on too many inscrutable notions. Freud has stated that a mother is happy on giving birth to a male child because he brings with him the penis longed for by the mother. This idea, plus such notions as a little boy's sexual desire for his mother or that all artists are merely manipulating feces, tend to shock one's "common sense." Psychoanalysis became so popular, not due to its nature, but because it had a good press image. Writers, says Salter, are probably among the most neurotic in the population. Upon hearing of a panacea for their troubles, they went for treatment in a big way. A rash of novels, plays, short stories, and newspaper articles resulted. The net result was a public relations campaign which eventually made it fashionable to be under analysis.[15]

A vital part of psychoanalysis is dream interpretation. Analytic dream theory can be criticized on a number of points. Salter writes that Freudian "myths" are just as false when dreamed as when discussed during the day. He denies that every dream displays a wish or that, as Freud has stated, all dreams are neurotic symptoms. The word association of dreams with sex is purely the result of a personal orientation rather than the truth. To demonstrate, Salter displays how he can draw an association between any two words in two or three linguistic steps. To the analysts, however, any linkage is the result of unconscious inclination. Freud's early belief that universal symbols are inherited from one's ancestors has been challenged as even more preposterous.[16]

Two further criticisms reported by Salter concern the analysand's tendency to avoid reality and become dependent on his analyst to help him solve everyday emotional problems. By searching into his past for clues to a behavioral oddity, the analysand is able to discount any current guilt and place the blame on something "over which he had no control." Finally, even if a psychotherapist helps one develop insight into his problems, this by no means ensures any improvement. For example, Salter quotes one of his acquaintances: "I have seen about twenty people at different times who have been thoroughly psychoanalyzed—at least they said so—and that convinced me against analysis more than any theoretical objections."[17]

Pinckney has severely criticized psychoanalysis on a number of grounds. In the preface to one of his books, he writes that it (the book) "is meant to be no more than my own expression of horror at the plight of so many innocent people being victimized by 'pretenders' of the healing arts."[18] Due to the psychoanalyst's tendency to look for an emotional cause of mental illness, many organic diseases are overlooked. A brain tumor, for example, can cause depression, assaultive behavior, and paranoid symptoms. Much organic illness is mistaken for psychiatric illness and, as such, leads to needless suffering and even premature death. One concerned doctor closely re-examined 115 patients who had been diagnosed as neurotic or having other mental problems. He found that all had a physical disease. After the correct diagnosis had been made, 45 were cured, 36 improved, 3 remained unchanged and 31 died; 25 of the deaths were from cancer that had been overlooked by psychiatrists.[19]

Pinckney writes that, in addition to overlooking physical causes for erratic behavior, many psychiatrists encourage their analysands to do things which express their freedom from repression. In demonstrating this new-found "freedom," the analysand begins to feel guilty. The therapist then spends time working on curing this newly created guilt. Although he only quotes from those cases known to him personally, Pinckney places the blame for numerous divorces on psychoanalytic "advice." According to Pinckney's view of the Freudian outlook on the man-and-wife relationship, if one functions harmoniously with his spouse, then he leads a dull and mundane life. One quote from Freud reads, "Whoever is to be really free and happy in love must have overcome his deference for women and come to terms with the idea of incest with mother or sister."[20]

There are no adequate governmental regulations regarding the licensing or practicing of psychoanalysis. Various institutes offer psychoanalytic training approved by the American Psychoanalytic Association. The American Psychoanalytic Association, however, has no "official" recognition in the professional, medical, or legal world. The American Medical Association refuses to define, in detail, what it considers necessary psychoanalytic training to be. Under the laws of most states, legally and professionally, anyone can call himself a psychoanalyst if he so chooses. Psychoanalysts undergo analysis themselves as a part of their "academic training." If they fail to perform as expected by the "training" analyst, their training may terminate. Thus, the practice has a selective attraction. As for the standard "four year psychoanalytic curriculum," many institutes do not require student participation in more than two, two-hour sessions per week (the total amount of study comes to a bit more than half the hours needed to complete second grade).[21]

Other scholars have written harshly of psychoanalysis, particularly of the classical model. To quote Harry Wells, "It acts as a misleading body of ideas and establishes blocks in the path of knowledge and progress."[22] Such bitter criticisms of psychoanalysis have extended to the entire practice of psychotherapy. This generalization is due to the fact that a great proportion of therapists have adopted basically Freudian notions. Furthermore, psychotherapy often operates on principles of interpretation and association and, as a result, is open to most of the same personal biases as psychoanalysis.

H. J. Eysenck has concluded that "There is no satisfactory evidence that psychotherapy benefits people suffering from neurotic conditions."[23] He examined the published reports of the effects of psychotherapy performed on 7,293 patients and wrote that the evidence fails to prove that psychotherapy, Freudian or otherwise, facilitates the recovery of neurotic patients. In fact, the evidence tends to indicate that roughly two-thirds of a group of neurotic patients will recover or improve to a marked extent within two years of the onset of their illness, whether they are treated by psychotherapy or not. This figure appears relatively stable from one investigation to another, regardless of type of treatment used or type of patient treated. P. G. Denker reached similar conclusions after studying the case histories of five hundred patients receiving disability payments because of neurotic disturbances severe enough to keep them from work. These individuals were treated by private physicians untrained in psychotherapy. Despite this fact, a two year follow-up showed that 72 percent of the patients resumed work and had not felt the need to ask for further help.[24] It might be noted that this "spontaneous remission" is somewhat higher than the two-thirds improvement rate generally reported by psychotherapists.

Eysenck argues that neurotic behavior is learned behavior. As the result of some traumatic event, a previously neutral stimulus, through association, becomes connected with the unconditioned stimuli which gives rise to the traumatic, emotional reactions. From that point on, both conditioned and unconditioned stimuli produce the original maladaptive behavior. Where conditioned responses are not reinforced, they begin to extinguish. Ergo, spontaneous remission occurs. Where recovery does not occur, it is because the individual has continued to reinforce his neurotic responses through a process of operant conditioning.[25]

According to a recent publication by R. B. Stuart, iatrogenic illness is a not uncommon phenomenon. The term "iatrogenic" refers to something brought about by the treatment of a physician. Stuart reports a study where it is estimated that up to twenty percent of the medical patients in one sample suffered from illnesses with iatrogenic complications.[26] Although there is far less literature on the iatrogenic factors in psychiatric treatment than in purely medical treatment and diagnosis, evidence is mounting that psychotherapy can be dangerous. In one study of 143 male veterans, psychiatric hospitalization operated to intensify feelings of decline and impotence and to release aggressive and sexual impulses. Another study revealed that, while two groups of in-patients seem to have benefited from psychotherapy, long-term psychotics deteriorated during its course. The most alarming aspect of this study was the finding that long-term psychotic controls showed a large positive change during the same period.[27] Stuart launches an attack against psychiatric hospitalization by documenting several studies which indicate that at least 75 percent of those persons hospitalized are not in need of hospitalization, as determined by their ability to remain in the community following denial of hospitalization or treatment in hospitals for only very brief periods.

Treatment of a psychiatric patient is often more dependent on idiosyncratic needs of the staff and institutional convenience (bed-space, etc.) than on the patient's diagnosed condition. A well-documented study by Hollingshead and Redlich established a correlation between kinds of treatment and diagnoses and the social class of the patient.[28] Diagnostic labels attached to psychiatric patients serve to stigmatize them, sociologically and psychologically, and gravitate against cure. Stuart also questions the reliability of psychiatric diagnoses. In summarizing several studies presented to the reader, he states that psychiatric diagnoses and clinical judgments, which generally depend upon the identification of dispositional characteristics, have not demonstrated a high level of reliability. He attributes this lack of reliability to weaknesses in the conception of the diagnostic typologies and to other factors inherent in the situations in which judgments are made. This view is supported by Cronbach in an overview of psychiatric evaluations and predictions. Psychiatric evaluations of an individual's performance were poorer than test information in one experiment while, in another experiment, psychiatrists were unable to predict much better than chance those personalities which would be successful in pilot training.[29]

Several criticisms of psychiatry in general have been voiced by Thomas Szasz, himself a psychiatrist. In essence, Szasz argues that psychiatry dehumanizes man because it denies him, on the basis of spurious scientific reasoning, the existence or possibility of personal responsibility. By accepting such notions as the "dictatorship of the unconscious," man's sentient and independent psyche is disputed. In many cases, according to Szasz, individuals are considered psychotic and so treated, not because they have lost contact with reality, but because their behavior is unpopular or "seems" abnormal. In other words, because an individual's behavior is disliked or misunderstood, he often becomes a candidate for psychiatric institutionalization. Szasz has likened mental hospitals to prisons and sees little difference between the two. Both serve the purpose of containing social undesirables except that, where hospitals are concerned, society can rationalize and say "We do our best" to help the unfortunate.[30]

Psychiatric terms are pathology oriented and are used primarily as invectives: their aim is to degrade. Should the psychiatrist be disputed on theoretical grounds, his retort is often the quick diagnosis of his opponent as a paranoid. Should he personally dislike a politician, the psychiatrist hides behind a tirade of psychological invectives rather than a value estimate. Not only can such a quick and easy "diagnosis" do much to harm the individual, its main thrust is to collectivize man, to deprive him of idiosyncrasy by referring to any and all deviation as pathology.[31]

FOOTNOTES

1. Merle M. Ohlsen, *Group Counseling* (New York: Holt, Rinehart and Winston, Inc., 1970), pp. 1-2.
2. Jane Warters, *Group Guidance* (New York: McGraw-Hill Book Company, Inc., 1960), p. 170.
3. *ibid.*, p. 173.
4. Robert W. White, *The Abnormal Personality* (3rd ed.; New York: The Ronald Press, 1964), pp. 283-287.
5. *ibid.*, pp. 289-304.
6. Based on a survey of 18,026 psychologists by the National Science Foundation in 1966, Ross Stagner and Charles M. Solley, *Basic Psychology: A Perceptual-Homeostatic Approach* (New York: McGraw-Hill Book Company, 1970), pp. 32-33.
7. U. S. Department of Labor, *Occupational Outlook Handbook*, Bulletin No. 1650 (Washington, D. C.: U. S. Government Printing Office, 1970-71), pp. 251-252.
8. William Gerber, "Future of Psychiatry," *Editorial Research Reports*, I (February, 1969), p. 128.
9. *ibid.*, pp. 125-126.
10. Ohlsen, *op. cit.*, p. 9.
11. *ibid.*, p. 273.
12. G. M. Gazda and Mary J. Larsen, "A Comprehensive Appraisal of Group and Multiple Counseling," *Journal of Research and Development in Education*, I (Winter, 1968), pp. 57-132.
13. Andrew Salter, *The Case Against Psychoanalysis* (New York: Henry Holt and Company, 1952), p. 2.
14. *ibid.*, p. 46.
15. *ibid.*, p. 11.
16. *ibid.*, pp. 54-92.
17. *ibid.*, p. 145.
18. Edward R. Pinckney and Cathy Pinckney, *The Fallacy of Freud and Psychoanalysis* (Englewood Cliffs: Prentice-Hall, Inc., 1965), p. iv.

19. *ibid.*, p. 10l.
20. *ibid.*, p. 130.
21. *ibid.*, p. 27.
22. Harry K. Wells, *The Failure of Psychoanalysis* (New York: International Publishers, 1963), p. 75.
23. H. J. Eysenck and S. Rachman, *The Causes and Cures of Neurosis* (London: Routledge & Kegan Paul, 1965), p. 268.
24. P. G. Denker, "Results of Treatment of Psychoneurosis by the General Practitioner: A Follow-up Study of 500 Cases," *New York State Journal of Medicine*, XLVI (1946), pp. 2164-66.
25. Eysenck and Rachman, *op. cit.*, pp. 1-13.
26. Richard B. Stuart, *Trick or Treatment: How and When Psychotherapy Fails* (Champaign: Research Press, 1970), pp. 10-11.
27. *ibid.*, p. 24.
28. See August B. Hollingshead and Frederick Redlich, *Social Class and Mental Illness* (New York: John Wiley & Sons, 1958).
29. Lee J. Cronbach, *Essentials of Psychological Testing* (3rd ed.; New York: Harper & Row, 1970), pp. 674-675.
30. Thomas S. Szasz, *Ideology and Insanity* (New York: Doubleday & Comapny, Inc., 1970), pp. 113-139.
31. *ibid.*, p. 30.

VIII. CONCLUSIONS AND IMPLICATIONS

A. CONTRADICTIONS IN THE LITERATURE

The preceding pages have endeavored to survey the nature, extent, and efficacy of resocialization programs in three major institutional areas: education, criminolegal systems, and industry. The practices of counseling and psychotherapy, so often included in resocialization efforts, were also analyzed. That there exists a great deal of variety and contradiction in the literature related to resocialization seems to be a major finding of this research.

Educators have attributed the causes of learning disability to a number of factors. While all seem to agree that learning disability can be caused by the physiology of the individual, there is disagreement over the relative importance of other aspects of the individual's sociological, psychological, and institutional life. Where some authors emphasize cultural differences and prejudices as a major cause of learning difficulties, others look to the motivations and perceptions of the individual. The institutional practices of education have also been challenged as harmful to learning. Critics have argued that irrelevant curricula, teaching methods, and teacher attitudes play a large part in the etiology of learning disability. Few adherents to any particular theory of learning disability unequivocally reject all other theories. It seems well accepted that many of the causes are closely related and, for other than analytical purposes, cannot be separated. There appears to be a tremendous polarity, however, between those who regard compensatory education as successful and those who consider it largely ineffective. That the educators are qualified to make assessments is not disputed. The academic and experimental backgrounds of those on both sides of the issue seem irreproachable. Looking to the research designs of the various studies also seems fruitless. No side seems to have demonstrated a methodology superior to the other. Nevertheless, the adherents of compensatory education continue to present evidence purporting to document learning improvement while the detractors report that learning improvement is nil or, at best, only temporary.

The nature of crime and criminal rehabilitation has also been disputed. Criminal behavior has been attributed to innate, inherited deficiencies in the individual or to power conflicts between social classes. Semanticists have argued that a man becomes a criminal only through definition, not necessarily through act. While these explanations may have varying degrees of truth in them, psychological and sociological theories of criminal etiology are most popular.

Some scientists look to the psyche of the individual for explanations of criminal behavior. The psychological school of thought purports to explain a person's criminal behavior through analysis of his personality. Character disorders, ego dependency, and other psychopathologies have been considered criminogenic. The sociological school looks to the pressures of the social system to find an explanation for criminal behavior. Peer-group pressures are considered crucial to the development of that behavior judged deviant by the dominant society. In recent years, the psychological and sociological schools have tended to converge, each school making increased allowance for the findings of the other.

In the area of criminal rehabilitation, this synthesis is also visible. Most authorities agree that diagnosed personality problems must be dealt with if rehabilitation is to take place. Allegiances to peer-group values must also be considered in any resocialization program. Notwithstanding the cooperative effort of both schools of thought, the efficacy of criminal rehabilitation is being severely questioned. For every report of a satisfactory rehabilitation program, evidence of high recidivism is placed in opposition. Some authors write of delinquency reduction through intensive casework while others have argued that such intensive care actually increases violation rates. Rehabilitation programs similar in design and implementation will often produce divergent results. Although theories pertaining to rehabilitation seem highly logical when developed on paper, they are contradicted by the prevalence of recidivists in our correctional institutions.

Training for the hard-core unemployed has received increased attention during the past decade. Social scientists exploring the predicament of the chronically unemployed have found two areas of explanation. Due to prejudice and various economic reasons, the objective job situation for the Negro, Mexican-American, and southern Appalachian has been quite limited. Members of certain minority groups have been denied job entrance or, if given work, they have been restricted to the most menial labor. These conditions have been instrumental in placing many individuals in such a subjective state of mind that, even if offered substantial jobs, they would be psychologically unable to hold them. Poor self-image, insecurity, and undeveloped working skills gravitate against successful occupational adjustment.

To mitigate the plight of the hard-core unemployed a two-pronged attack has been advocated. Industry is being prodded to equalize job opportunities and to provide for job upgrading and advancement for all. Coupled with this improvement in the objective situation, concern is being expressed for the sociological and psychological adjustment of the hard-core unemployed. Concentrated training, supportive psychological services, and increased tolerance for tardiness and absenteeism are incorporated into most training programs. Every effort is made to understand the disadvantaged individual and to help his industrial development. The results of training for the hard-core remain unclear. Numerous companies have reported high rates of success with their programs while others experience high turnover and low morale. Where the human resources council for one city lauds training efforts, officials in another urban area claim mismanagement and inefficacy. There appears to be a great deal of contradiction between various program evaluations and, to date, no one has been able to understand why.

Counseling and psychotherapy are employed quite extensively in resocialization programs. Many authorities in the field of behavior intervention argue that supportive psychological services are needed by the remedial student, criminal recidivist, and hard-core unemployed if effective behavior modification is to take place. Counseling and psychotherapy vary in intensity and technique. The basic principle of both, however, is based on the identification and acceptance of personal problems through the aid of supportive and therapeutic interpersonal relationships. To this end, counselors and psychotherapists play a large role in resocialization programs.

While the need for supportive psychological services appears to be generally accepted, there is mounting evidence that current practices are largely ineffective. Although the popular media such as television and motion pictures appear rather intrigued with psychoanalysis and psychotherapy, many concerned professionals are less than enthusiastic. Some studies not only challenge the efficacy of psychotherapy, they claim it can be harmful to the individual. By ignoring organic origins of neurotic behavior, and through the use of pathologically-oriented interpretations, psychiatrists often do more harm than good.

Thus, there appears to be a great deal of contradiction in the literature related to resocialization. For every successful program, there is a failure. For every professional who considers resocialization effective there is one who criticizes its inefficacy. Similar programs aimed at similar clientele and carried out in a similar manner are sometimes regarded as failures, sometimes as successes. If the theoretical bases of resocialization are presumed sound and, if it is assumed that subjective and objective factors are held constant, then contradiction stems from the interpretation of results rather than from the results themselves.

B. A METHOD OF INTERPRETATION

One way to interpret the contradictions in the literature

is to explore the possible reasons why reported findings might be in error. Although this method involves no original clinical observation and relies on inference, it provides perspective on both sides of the issue. Errors in research findings can be involuntary or voluntary (defined as the absence or existence of personal will). This analysis will begin with a discussion of possible involuntary and voluntary errors in those findings which indicate that resocialization is failing.

Resocialization programs are often planned and staffed by relatively well-educated members of the middle class. The subjects of resocialization programs, however, are generally members of the lower class and subscribe to the values of a different subculture. This divergency in culture often results in a breakdown in communication between the two classes. Class ethnocentrism and personal antagonisms further impede communication.

Standard research problems must also be considered. Systematic error, the result of poor research design, and chance error, the encountering of purely arbitrary data, often contribute to erroneous findings. Failure to report progress in resocialization due to the above reasons would constitute involuntary error.

Voluntary falsification of research findings may also occur. Many resocialization programs involve a high percentage of ethnic and racial minority group members. Bigots have been known to go to extreme lengths to keep their victims from receiving social and economic benefits. By falsely reporting the failure of one resocialization program, a prejudiced individual contributes to the cancellation of future programs. Resocialization might also be termed a failure, not because it really is, but because the reporter holds different priorities. There are those who consider space exploration or foreign expansion to be more important or more practical than resocialization. By providing evidence that resocialization is failing, they work to alter the commitment of government monies. Failure to report progress in resocialization due to these reasons would constitute voluntary error.

Those studies which report successful resocialization may also be analyzed in terms of involuntary and voluntary errors. Behavior change as the result or consequence of treatment and/or study has often been noted. In some cases, however, further research indicated that the perceived change in behavior was artificial and temporary and that the individual returned to his previous pattern of behavior. In the "Hawthorne Studies," investigators studied the assumption that physical conditions affect work output. This theory was put to the test and the linear relationship between the two held. When objective work conditions were made poorer, however, work output continued to rise. The fact that the workers knew they were part of an experiment affected their performance.[1] In those instances where behavior alters as the result of observation rather than the manipulation of independent variables, regression to the previous norm will occur after the termination of treatment. In many resocialization programs, particularly in those where participation is voluntary, the "Hawthorne effect" must be considered in any interpretation of the findings.

A closely related phenomenon is termed the "hello-goodbye" effect. When entering a resocialization program or therapeutic relationship, many subjects feel a subtle social pressure to discuss personal problems (in order to justify their presence in the program). When they wish to terminate participation, they often feel a social obligation to express gratitude and satisfaction. In other words, some subjects overemphasize their problems when "going in" and overemphasize their adjustment when "coming out." Essentially, the subjects are careful to tell the counselor or therapist what they think he wants to hear.[2] This type of response pattern seriously challenges the validity of program evaluations.

Systematic and chance error play the same role in relation to positive reports as they do to negative reports. Where research design is inadequate or where chance data are not controlled for, experimental results are unlikely to be valid. Perhaps the major criticism relating to the design and evaluation of resocialization programs is the failure to control for two extraneous variables: history and maturation. As will be discussed, this omission often leads to the postulation of spurious cause-effect relationships.

Even where resocialization programs are considered an over-all failure, there appear to be certain individuals who have been resocialized. This change is generally attributed to the treatment process. When resocialization programs are considered successful, all improvement is attributed to intervention. Actually, however, if a person's behavior has truly been altered, the historical variable rather than the treatment may have been the cause. Between the start and finish of a resocialization program, many other change-producing events may have occurred in addition to the program itself. While participating in resocialization programs, subjects may be exposed to improved socio-economic conditions, promising political campaigns, and any number of varying social conditions. Should their behavior change, it could be the result of these events rather than the resocialization program.

A second variable is maturation. This term applies to those biological and psychological processes which systematically vary with the passage of time and are independent of specific external events. Thus, between the start and finish of a program, the subjects may have grown older, wiser, more tired, more bored, etc. Any difference in behavior may reflect this process rather than the resocialization activities. In dealing with remedial education students, for example, "spontaneous remission" (as discussed in Chapter VII), may be mistaken for the specific effect of remedial treatment. Such a remission is not "spontaneous" in any causal sense, but rather represents the effects of learning processes and environmental pressures of daily experience which would be operating even if no behavior intervention had taken place.[3]

To sum up, it appears that many individuals alter their behavior as a result of objective and subjective factors totally unrelated to their involvement in resocialization programs. Where these programs report success, it is highly possible that the subjects would have altered their behavior along the desired lines anyway. Failure to recognize this fact is responsible for much involuntary error.

There are two major explanations for research findings

which report success in resocialization when, indeed, there has been no observed change in values, attitudes, or abilities. The first source of voluntary error relates to "vested interests." Generally, the same personnel who operate various resocialization programs participate in evaluating them. Internal evaluations predominate because, at first, it seems quite logical that personnel directly involved with resocialization would be in the best position to assess results. It should be noted, however, that those who conduct these evaluations stand to lose not only their professional reputations but their jobs if they do not find evidence that resocialization is effective. If compensatory education, criminal rehabilitation, training for the hard-core, and psychotherapy prove ineffective, what need is there for remedial teachers, social workers, vocational counselors, and psychotherapists? Asking for objective evaluations from these people is tantamount to asking a man to testify against himself.[4]

A second explanation for voluntary error in reporting relates to political consequences. As mentioned earlier, many resocialization programs involve a high percentage of members of various racial and ethnic minorities. Given the current emphasis on universal suffrage, equalitarianism, and support of the "underdog," to report that resocialization is failing could mean the end of certain political careers. Rather than risk alienation of various minority groups, the white liberal, and the mass media, many program directors and their political allies seek to make findings on resocialization more palatable to the public. Suppression of scientific findings and threats on the lives of scientists are quite possible even in this "enlightened" age. The government supression of the "Coleman Report" and the numerous threats on the life of Dr. Arthur Jensen stand in evidence. Scientific "truth" is, it seems, directly related to the socio-political mood of the times.[5]

C. THE QUESTION OF RESOCIALIZATION

Considering the issues discussed in the previous section, it seems safe to assume that resocialization is not an unqualified success. In fact, the evidence casts doubt as to whether resocialization is even a possibility. Further considerations on the nature of resocialization may help to clarify the issue.

Essentially, resocialization is the altering of an individual's values, attitudes, and abilities as the result of outside intervention. Where values, attitudes, and abilities change independently of outside intervention, it cannot be said that *re*socialization has taken place. Instead, the individual has continued to socialize himself and has developed according to his own internal patterns. Whatever the cause, values, attitudes, and abilities (the acquisition of which depends on values and attitudes) are slow in changing. This is reflected in the common idiom by such sayings as: "You cannot teach an old dog new tricks"; "A leopard doesn't change his spots"; and, "Once a liar, always a liar." Although these statements cannot be considered as scientific observations of human behavior, more sophisticated social theorists have given evidence that resocialization is a very difficult proposition.

The fact that learning experiences are very crucial early in one's life seems widely accepted. Ideas and attitudes inculcated early in childhood or adolescence become more and more consistent as the individual matures.[6] Once idiosyncratic attitudes and behavior develop a pattern of reinforcement and stabilization, only a drastic application of stimuli will bring about relatively rapid change. Kenneth Bolding writes that, ". . . our image is in itself resistant to change. When it receives messages which conflict with it, its first impulse is to reject them as in some sense untrue." [7] Some social scientists are of the opinion that fundamental value and attitude changes would require several generations and would have to begin with the youth of each generation.[8] Although he called it re-education, Kurt Lewin considered value and attitude change so difficult that, unless undertaken in an extremely enlightened manner, it would be virtually impossible.[9]

Considering the empirical, idiomatic, and theoretical evidence that current resocialization programs are failing, one wonders why society continues to support existing programs or initiate new ones based on the same practices as the old. The answer is a "fear of the alternative." Few parents or spouses want to hear that loved ones cannot be cured by psychotherapy. Society does not want to believe that is can do little to stop some of its members from destroying it from within. To accept that resocialization is failing is to lose hope. According to one psychologist, to lose hope is to approach suicide, be it individual or societal.[10]

D. THE PROMISE OF THE FUTURE

1. The Nature of Behavior Therapy

Although resocialization does not appear to be highly successful, human behavior continues to change. The fact that a teacher, social worker, vocational instructor, or psychiatrist might be unable to intervene successfully in an individual's behavior does not mean that the behavior patterns of an individual will not alter. The notion of "spontaneous remission" can be applied in the social sphere. An individual may gradually come to acquire those values, attitudes, and abilities considered appropriate by the dominant institutions. This acquisition of traits comes about as a result of extraneous variables such as history and maturation, not necessarily as a result of the machinations of a given resocialization program. On the other hand, history and maturation (i.e., continuing socialization), often function to reinforce or even intensify precisely those attributes which cause an individual to be defined as inadequate by the dominant institutions.

Society generally chooses not to wait for an individual to alter his behavior as the result of continuing socialization. The mother of a poor reader, criminal son, or disturbed daughter may seek ways to change behavior within a relatively brief period of time. This is a crucial difference between continuing socialization and resocialization. Resocialization seeks to do rapidly what continuing socialization may only do eventually (or not at all).[11]

Whereas   humanistic,   interpersonal   approaches   to

resocialization have not proven successful, there is increasing evidence that a behavioral approach may be more effective. Behavior therapy is based on fundamental learning theory. Any given response will increase in frequency if positively reinforced or decrease in frequency if punished. Behavior which evokes no stimulus whatsoever eventually begins to disappear or extinguish. By punishing one type of behavior and by rewarding another, more or less permanent behavior modification may take place. Punishment and reward are not restricted to the notion of conscious pain or pleasure. Whatever stimulus decreases a preceding response is punishment. Whatever stimulus increases a preceding response is reward. For a learning bond to be created, however, reinforcement should be immediate and consistent. Although this book cannot investigate thoroughly the nature and principles of behavior therapy, a few examples of this form of treatment are provided.

Eysenck cites the case of a thirty-three-year-old man who had uncontrollable impulses to attack prams and handbags since the age of ten. Whenever possible, he would somehow damage perambulators or scratch purses. Psychotherapy helped him to trace the origins of this behavior to childhood. One day after sailing a toy sailboat at the park, he accidentally hit a pram with the boat as he was taking it out of the water. The feminine consternation expressed by the pram's owner excited him. Not long after, he began to feel a sexual thrill when handling his sister's purse. Although psychotherapy helped him realize how his fetish began, he continued to feel sexual impulses at the sight of these objects. Knowing the source of his behavior was not sufficient to eliminate it. The subject's psychiatrist finally recommended he undergo surgery for a prefrontal lobotomy.

Rather than having this surgery, the patient was hospitalized and given behavior therapy. The patient was shown a collection of handbags and perambulators after he had received an injection of apomorphine and just before nausea was produced. This treatment was given several times daily for a nine-day period. The patient reported that he no longer required the use of fantasies to have intercourse with his wife and no longer felt compelled to attack prams and purses. Nevertheless, the treatment was continued until the mere sight of his former sexual objects made him sick. After treatment ceased, the patient's marital and social adjustment eventually became exemplary.[12]

Behavior therapy employs positive reinforcement as well as aversive consequences. In one research project, a number of socially and academically deviant male elementary school children were placed in an experimental classroom and subjected to behavior therapy. Although all of these students were of average or above average intelligence, they presented extreme behavior problems and would not complete academic assignments. The idea of the study was to increase the amount of academic task-oriented behavior and reduce "acting out" behavior. The classroom functioned on a token-economy system. Students were given points for task-oriented behavior as well as for amount of work produced. These points could be exchanged for "free time," wherein students were allowed to engage in such rewarding behavior as building model cars, listening to music, etc. Where antisocial behavior was exhibited, aversion therapy was employed. Whenever a child disrupted class, he was removed from the classroom and isolated for a period of time in an adjoining room. At the end of seven weeks of behavior therapy, social behavior improved and the mean amount of task-oriented time increased from a baseline of 50 percent to 84 percent.[13]

Behavior therapy has its drawbacks. With this form of treatment, total control of a subject's environment is needed in order to ensure that punishment and reward can be administered when appropriate and on a regular and consistent basis. Probably the greatest drawback to behavior therapy, however, is public opinion. Many individuals look on behavior therapy as cruel and dehumanizing. They object to treating human beings as "laboratory animals." They feel that punishment is too harsh and that the use of rewards is hypocritical. It is possible that those who view behavior therapy in this light are more concerned with upholding their own morality than they are with improving a given subject's condition. As long as they feel they are doing the "just" thing, they are able to accept society's relative inability to resocialize. What the detractors of behavior therapy fail to realize is that their insistence on "moral means" may lead to failure to achieve "ends." In this situation, the potential recovery of a diviant individual is sacrificed because the public does not think his therapeutic treatment would comply with its values.

2. Resocializing the Current Generation

Perhaps the best way to achieve resocialization would be to de-emphasize the humanistic approach to human behavior and emphasize the pragmatism of learning theory. In the educational institution, students should be immediately punished when they violate institutional norms and immediately rewarded when they adhere to them. Instead, academic inadequacy is rewarded by allowing deviant children increased study-hall time, more nonacademic courses, relaxed discipline, and eventually, a high school diploma based on seniority rather than ability. If the purpose of the educational institution is learning, this process should be returned to the direction of educational professionals rather than left to the caprice of immature students or uninformed parents. Education should be taken out of the political arena and rededicated to the task of developing student intellect. Rather than first considering the political consequences of an educational policy, its impact on learning should be evaluated.

Many school systems operate on the humanistic assumption that students should be allowed to progress according to their own interests. To assume that children or adolescents need only internal motivation to learn is to sacrifice pragmatism for fad. As for college programs, disadvantaged students should not be advanced until they perform at proper level. To push them through college as they were pushed through high school will lead to the same tragic consequences.

Criminal rehabilitation could be made far more effective

by emphasizing the tenets of learning theory. Where it is determined that a form of punishment (aversion therapy) is necessary, said punishment should be administered immediately and consistently. Instead, juveniles are often allowed to commit several crimes before action is taken against them. If only treated for the fifth crime, but not for the previous four, the juvenile will not associate response with stimulus. The follies of the legal system carry over to adult courts. Due to crowded dockets and maneuvering defense attorneys, many trials are not terminated for months after they were begun. There is little foundation in learning theory for applying punishment long after an act was committed. In cases where it is applied, no learning takes place. Many judges know this and therefore release the criminal on probation. Thus, no action at all is taken to deter further crime. In effect, the criminal act is rewarded.

For some unknown reason, judges still have power to sentence. In light of the fact that judges must function as lawyers, accountants, bookkeepers, and politicians, it is difficult to understand why they are expected to know what rehabilitative alternative is best for a man. As lawyers, they should see that due process is carried out. That is all their academic and experiential background has trained them for. If a man is found guilty, his sentence should be determined by a panel of experts. Due to their academic and clinical knowledge of human behavior, psychologists, probation officers, and others who have dealt with criminal rehabilitation should have power of sentence.

Treatment of the deviant individual is usually determined more by politics and self-concern than by pragmatism. Depending on the political mood of the times, judges are overly harsh or overly lenient, and the inconsistencies of their sentences are notorious. The use of methadone, which has by no means proven to be "the answer" to the problem of drug addiction, has been greatly expanded in all our major cities. The millions of dollars being expended in this area constitute more of a political placebo than a true effort to get at the problem. Judges and members of the mass media are more concerned with upholding their own notions of morality than with effecting criminal rehabilitation. Rather than being solely concerned with a man's civil rights, they should be more concerned with his rights to live. Whereas custodial supervision may have saved them, many men have been released into the community to die, be killed, or commit even more serious offenses.

Training for the hard-core unemployed should be conducted according to learning theory. An individual who actively partakes in industrial training should be duly rewarded. Those who do not should not be rewarded. Nevertheless, they are. In many states, mature and healthy young men in their twenties are eligible for and receive welfare. All they need do is walk into a social service office and say they need money. They are given food and rent money for as long as they need it. If this practice must continue, these recipients should be required to partake in some form of vocational training so that, in the future, they might possess adequate job skills.

The abuse of unemployment compensation should also be stopped. Many individuals, upon receiving their first unemployment check, promptly stop looking for work. Since they are often guaranteed six months of a comfortable, tax-free income, they feel no motivation to gain employment or acquire job skills. As with welfare, able unemployment recipients should be required either to look for work daily or enroll in a government sponsored skills-development program.

Where counseling is deemed necessary, it should be used for informational, problem-solving purposes rather than for soul-searching. Most of the disadvantaged prefer hard facts and pragmatic approaches to problematic situations. It is generally the counselors who prefer to employ the moral-philosophical approach. Rather than spending thousands of dollars to please members of the press and a few members of the community, money should be put directly to work.[14] Most federally and state funded projects hire "community people" to act as liaison and information officers. Their job is to "rap" on the grassroots level and effect government-citizen cooperation. While all this seems logical on paper, it is largely a waste of money. A time-study evaluation of these jobs would reveal that many individuals actually "work" only a few hours a week. Considering the fact that salaries for these "vital" positions often range from 15 to 30 thousand dollars a year, it is again obvious that pragmatism is sacrificed to politics. Rather than spending this money on salaries, ghetto children should be provided the dental and medical care they need.

To sum up, if resocialization programs are to be effective, they must be operated along more pragmatic lines. Humanistic rationalizations and political intrigues should not supercede the tenets of learning theory. The air must be cleared. If society expects its members to function according to institutional norms, then desirable behavior must be clearly, consistently, and immediately rewarded. Undesirable behavior must either be ignored or punished. People in powerful political positions and influential members of the mass media must begin to worry more about the efficacy of resocialization than about upholding their idiosyncratic sense of morality. They must be willing to sacrifice political office and financial gain. Instead of telling the public what they think it wants to hear, they should work to produce the results the public expects.

3. Socializing the Next Generation

If the initial process of socialization had been more effective, many individuals would not find themselves placed in resocialization programs. Since resocialization is generally so difficult to achieve, it seems logical that more attention should be devoted to perfecting socialization. In contemporary society, however, we expend time and energy when it is usually far too late.

Due to certain moral-philosophic notions, the family is considered to be so inviolable that, although the processes within it may be socially internecine, institutional intervention is discouraged. Even if parents, or parent, have consistently demonstrated an inability to socialize their offspring, no societal action is taken. The incidence of fatherless homes has so increased in our cities that it is commonplace to find a mother left alone with the task of rearing anywhere from one to twelve children. Although effective socialization is difficult under such conditions, the government seems to provide incentive for family expansion by guaranteeing the support of each and every unborn child. Those who believe that such dysfunctional family arrangements should be left alone are, once again, more concerned with their own principles than with the future of the disadvantaged. By taking a "liberal" approach to the fertility of welfare mothers, society is virtually forcing a child to grow up with too many siblings, too little motherly attention, and too little money.

Any society which cannot provide for the effective socialization of its children is doomed. The family, not our other social institutions, is primarily responsible for social "failures." Because the family is failing, the quality of life in our cities and suburbs is diminishing. Wherever lower, middle, or upper-class parents prove incapable of rearing their children, society must step in to accomplish the task. Two things must be done immediately. First, a system of community-operated "kibbutzim" should be established to provide for the socialization of children who would otherwise be doomed to a life of educational disability, imprisonment, or chronic unemployment. Second, any and all forms of institutional prejudice and racism must be rooted out in order to destroy the initial causes of family failure. This done, society will no longer need kibbutzim and the family will again be able to serve its social purpose.

FOOTNOTES

1. F. J. Roethlisberger and W. J. Dickson, *Management and the Worker* (Cambridge: Harvard University Press, 1939).
2. S. R. Hathaway, "Some Considerations Relative to Nondirective Psychotherapy as Counseling," *Journal of Clinical Psychology*, IV (July, 1968), p. 228.
3. Donald T. Campbell and Julian C. Stanley, *Experimental and Quasi-Experimental Designs for Research* (Chicago: Rand McNally & Company, 1966), pp. 7-9.
4. Walter B. Miller, "Inter-Institutional Conflict As a Major

Impediment to Delinquency Prevention," in *Juvenile Delinquency: A Book of Readings*, ed. by Rose Giallombardo (New York: John Wiley and Sons, Inc., 1966), p. 565.

5. Robert Ardrey, *The Social Contract* (New York: Atheneum, 1970), pp. 21-37.

6. Muzafer Sherif, *In Common Predicament* (New York: Houghton Mifflin Company, 1966), p. 31.

7. Kenneth Bolding, *The Image* (Ann Arbor: The University of Michigan Press, 1956), p. 8.

8. Sherif, *op. cit.*, p. 25.

9. Kurt Lewin, *Resolving Social Conflicts* (New York: Harper & Row, 1948), Chapter IV.

10. Maurice L. Farber, *Theory of Suicide* (New York: Funk & Wagnalls, 1968), pp. 12-27.

11. Leonard Broom and Philip Selznick, *Sociology: A Text with Adapted Readings* (4th ed.; New York: Harper and Row, 1968), p. 107.

12. H. J. Eysenck, *Crime and Personality* (Boston: Houghton Mifflin Company, 1964), pp. 154-156.

13. Robert L. Mattos, Robert H. Mattson, Hill M. Walker, and Nancy K. Buckley, "Reinforcement and Aversive Control in the Modification of Behavior," *Academic Therapy*, V (Fall, 1969), p. 45.

14. See Tom Wolfe, *Radical Chic & Mau-Mauing the Flak Catchers* (New York: Farrar, Straus & Giroux, 1970), pp. 95-153.

BIBLIOGRAPHY

Abraham, Willard. *The Slow Learner.* New York: The Center for Applied Research in Education, 1964.

Abrahamson, David. *The Psychology of Crime.* New York: John Wiley & Sons, Inc., 1960.

Ardrey, Robert. *The Social Contract.* New York, Atheneum, 1970.

Beck, John M. and Saxe, Richard W. *Teaching the Culturally Disadvantaged Pupil.* Springfield: Bannerstone House, 1965.

Berman, Louis. "Crime and the Endocrine Glands." *American Journal of Psychiatry,* XII (September, 1932), pp. 215-238.

Berne, Eric. *A Layman's Guide to Psychiatry and Psycho-Analysis.* 3rd ed. New York: Simon and Schuster, 1968.

Blight, Thomas. "Recidivism." *Encyclopedia Britannica.* 1965. Vol. XIX.

Bloom, Benjamin; Davis, Allison; and Hess, Robert, *Compensatory Education for Cultural Deprivation.* New York: Holt, Rinehart and Winston, Inc., 1965.

Blum, Albert A. and Schmidt, Charles T. "Job Training Through Adult Education: A Second Chance for the Negro and the Community." *Employment, Race and Poverty.* Edited by Arthur M. Ross and Herbert Hill. New York: Harcourt, Brace and World, Inc., 1967.

Bolding, Kenneth. *The Image.* Ann Arbor: The University of Michigan Press, 1956.

Breul, Frank R. "Early History of Aid to the Unemployed in the United States." *In Aid of the Unemployed.* Edited by Joseph M. Becker. Baltimore: The John Hopkins Press, 1965.

Brim, Orville G., Jr. "Adult Socialization." *Socialization and Society.* Edited by John Clausen. Boston: Little, Brown and Company, 1968.

Broom, Leonard and Selznick, Phillip. Sociology: *A Text with Adapted Readings.* 4th ed. New York: Harper & Row, 1968.

Brown, Roger. *Social Psychology.* New York: The Free Press, 1965.

Bullough, Vern L. "Streetwalking: Theory and Practice." *Saturday Review,* IIL (September 4, 1965), pp. 52-54.

Campbell, Donald T. and Stanley, Julian C. *Experimental and Quasi-Experimental Designs for Research.* Chicago: Rand McNally & Company, 1966.

Campbell, Roald; Cunningham, Luvern L.; and McPhee, Roderick F. *The Organization and Control of American Schools.* Columbus: Charles E. Merrill Publishing Company, 1965.

Channen, Gloria. "The More Effective Schools." *The Urban Review,* II (February, 1967), pp. 23-26.

Child, I. L. "Socialization." *The Handbook of Social Psychology*. Edited by G. Lindzey. Cambridge: Addison-Wesley Publishing Co., 1954.
Childs, John. *Education and Morals*. New York: Appleton-Century Crofts, Inc., 1950.
Clausen, John. "Social and Psychological Factors in Drug Addiction." *Law and Contemporary Problems*, XXII (Winter, 1957), pp. 35-51.
Clinard, Marshal B. *Sociology of Deviant Behavior*. New York: Rinehart & Company, Inc., 1957.
Cloward, Richard A. and Ohlin, Lloyd E. *Delinquency and Opportunity*. Glencoe: The Free Press, 1960.
Cohen, Albert K. *Delinquent Boys: The Culture of the Gang*. Glencoe: The Free Press, 1955.
Cohn, Alvin W. "Contemporary Correctional Practice: Science or Art?" *Federal Probation*, XXXIV (September, 1970), pp. 20-23.
Conant, James B. *Slums and Suburbs*. New York: McGraw-Hill Book Company, 1961.
Connors, Joy. "They're On Their Way." *American Education*, VI (June, 1970), pp. 23-25.
Conrad, John. *Crime and Its Correction*. Berkeley: University of California Press, 1965.
"Controversy Over the More Effective Schools: A Special Supplement." *Urban Review*, II (May, 1968), pp. 15-34.
Cooley, Charles H. *Human Nature and the Social Order*. New York: Shocken Books, Inc., 1964.
Cooley, Charles H. *Social Organization*. New York: Charles Scribner's Sons, 1909.
Cressey, Donald R. "Crime." *Contemporary Social Problems*. Edited by Robert K. Merton and Robert A. Nisbet. New York: Harcourt, Brace and World, Inc., 1961.
"Crime Expense Now Up to 51 Billions a Year," *U. S. News and World Report*, October 26, 1970, pp. 30-34.
Cronbach, Lee J. *Essentials of Psychological Testing*. 3rd ed. New York: Harper & Row, 1970.
Crow, L. D.; Murray, W. I.; and Smythe, H. H., eds. *Educating the Culturally Disadvantaged Child*. New York: David McKay, 1966.
Deese, James. *The Psychology of Learning*. 2nd ed. New York: McGraw-Hill Book Company, Inc., 1958.
Denker, P. G. "Results of Treatment of Psychoneurosis by the General Practitioner: A Follow-up Study of 500 Cases." *New York State Journal of Medicine*, XLVI (1946), pp. 2164-66.
Detroit News. March 12, 1970. p. 20A.
Diana, Lewis. "What is Probation?" *Probation and Parole: Selected Readings*. Edited by Robert M. Carter and Leslie T. Wilkins. New York: John Wiley & Sons, Inc., 1970.
Dizard, Jan E. "Why Should Negroes Work?" *Negroes and Jobs*. Edited by Ferman, Louis A.; Kornbluh, Joyce L.; and Miller, J. A. Ann Arbor: The University of Michigan Press, 1968.
Dollard, John. *Frustration and Aggression*. New Haven: Yale University Press, 1939.
Dressler, David. *Practice and Theory of Probation and Parole*. 2nd ed. New York: Columbia University Press, 1969.

Ðrob, Judah and Sheblak, Vernon. "Training the Hard-Core Unemployed." *Manpower*, I (January, 1969), pp. 28-30.
"18 Million Have Reading Woes." *Daily Tribune* (Royal Oak, Michigan). September 12, 1970.
"Employing Ghetto Workers: Nine Lessons of Experience." *Management Thinking*, July, 1968, pp. 5-6.
"Employing the Employables: What Companies are Finding." *U. S. News and World Report*, August 12, 1968, pp. 49-51.
Eysenck, H. J. and Rachman, S. *The Causes and Cures of Neurosis.* London: Routledge & Kegan Paul, 1965.
Eysenck, H. J. *Crime and Personality.* Boston: Houghton Mifflin Company, 1964.
Fantini, Mario D. and Weinstein, Gerald. *The Disadvantaged: Challenge to Education.* New York: Harper and Row, Inc., 1968.
Farber, Maurice. "The Analysis of National Character." *Personality and Social Systems.* Edited by Neil and William Smelser. New York: John Wiley and Sons, Inc., 1963.
Farber, Maurice L. *Theory of Suicide.* New York: Funk & Wagnalls, 1968.
"The First Work of These Times." *American Education*, I (April, 1965), pp. 13-20.
Fox, David J. "Evaluating the More Effective Schools." *Phi Delta Kappa*, IL (June, 1968), pp. 593-597.
Freeman, Roger A. "Dead End in American Education." *National Review*, XXI (January 14, 1969), pp. 22-24.
Friedenberg, E. Z. *The Vanishing Adolescent.* Boston: Beacon Press, 1959.
Gazda, G. M. and Larsen, Mary J. "A Comprehensive Appraisal of Group and Multiple Counseling." *Journal of Research and Development in Education*, I (Winter, 1968), pp. 57-132.
Gerber, William. "Future of Psychiatry." *Editorial Research Reports*, I (February, 1969), pp. 123-142.
Gibbons, Don C. *Changing the Lawbreaker: The Treatment of Delinquents and Criminals.* Englewood Cliffs: Prentice-Hall, Inc., 1965.
Glasser, William. *Schools Without Failure.* New York: Harper & Row, 1969.
Glueck, Sheldon and Eleanor. *Physique and Delinquency.* New York: Harper and Brothers, 1956.
Goffman, Erving. *Stigma.* New Jersey: Prentice-Hall, Inc., 1963.
Gordon, Edmund W. and Wilkerson, Doxey A. *Compensatory Education for the Disadvantaged.* New York: College Entrance Examination Board, 1966.
Gordon, Edmund W. "Is Compensatory Education Failing?" *College Board Review*, LXII (Winter, 1966-67), pp. 7-12, 25.
Goring, Charles. *The English Convict.* London: His Majesty's Stationery Office, 1913.
Greenwald, Harold. *The Call Girl.* New York: Ballantine Books, 1958.
Hall, Edward T. *The Silent Language.* Greenwich: Fawcett Publications, Inc., 1959.
"Hard-Core Program Will Widen Its Base." *Business Week*, November 15, 1969, pp. 41-42.

Harriman, Phillip L. *Handbook of Psychological Terms.* Totowa: Littlefield, Adams and Co., 1968.

Hartung, Frank. *Crime, Law and Society.* Detroit: Wayne State University Press, 1965.

Hathaway, S. R. "Some Considerations Relative to Nondirective Psychotherapy as Counseling." *Journal of Clinical Psychology,* IV (July, 1968), pp. 226-231.

Havighurst, Robert. "Who are the Socially Disadvantaged?" *The Disadvantaged Child: Issues and Innovations.* Edited by Joe L. Frost and Glenn R. Hawkes. Boston: Houghton Mifflin Company, 1966.

"Headstart for Children in the Slums." *American Education,* I (December, 1964/January, 1965), pp. 30-31.

Hechinger, F. M. "Integrated vs. Compensated." *New York Times,* February 26, 1967.

Herskovits, Melville J. *Man and His Works.* New York: Alfred A. Knopf, 1948.

Hilgard, Ernest R. *Introduction to Psychology.* 3rd ed. New York: Harcourt, Brace & World, Inc., 1962.

Himes, Joseph S. "Some Work-Related Cultural Deprivations of Lower-Class Negro Youths." *Negroes and Jobs.* Edited by Ferman, Louis A.; Kornbluh, Joyce L.; and Miller, J. A. Ann Arbor: The University of Michigan Press, 1968.

Hollingshead, August and Redlich, Frederick. *Social Class and Mental Illness.* New York: John Wiley & Sons, 1958.

Holt, John. *How Children Fail.* New York: Dell Publishing Co., Inc., 1964.

Hoover, J. Edgar. *Crime in the United States.* Uniform Crime Reports—1969. Washington, D. C.: Federal Bureau of Investigation, 1970.

Horton, Paul B. and Hunt, Chester L. *Sociology.* 2nd ed. New York: McGraw-Hill Book Company, 1964.

"In a Time of Layoffs; Trouble for the 'Hard-core'." *U. S. News and World Report,* July 13, 1970, pp. 24-26.

Inkeles, Alex and Levinson, Daniel. "National Character: The Study of Modal Personality and Sociocultural Systems." *Handbook of Social Psychology.* Vol. II. Edited by Gardiner Lindzey. Reading: Addison-Wesley, Inc., 1954.

Irish, Marian D. and Prothro, James W. *The Politics of American Democracy.* 2nd ed. Englewood Cliffs: Prentice-Hall, Inc., 1959.

Jensen, Arthur R. "How Much Can We Boost I.Q. and Scholastic Improvement?" *Harvard Educational Review,* XXXIX (Winter, 1969), pp. 1-123.

Kahl, Joseph. *The American Class Structure.* New York: Holt, Rinehart and Winston, 1965.

Kerber, August and Smith, Wilfred, eds. "The Functions of Mass Culture." *Educational Issues in a Changing Society.* Detroit: Wayne State University Press, 1968.

Kohl, Herbert. *36 Children.* New York: The New American Library, 1967.

Krech, David; Crutchfield, Richard S.; and Ballachey, Egerton L. *Individual in Society.* New York: McGraw-Hill Book Company, Inc., 1962.

Lamoreaux, William R. "Exploding Some Myths." *Michigan Challenge*, IX (September, 1969), pp. 10-13.

Lewin, Kurt. *Resolving Social Conflicts*. New York: Harper & Row, 1948.

Lewis, Oscar. *La Vida*. New York: Vintage Books, 1966.

Liebow, Elliot. *Tally's Corner*. Boston: Little, Brown and Company, 1967.

Lindesmith, Alfred. *The Addict and the Law*. New York: Random House, Inc., 1965.

Lindgren, Henry C. *Educational Psychology in the Classroom*. 3rd ed. New York: John Wiley & Sons, Inc., 1967.

Lombroso, Cesar. *L'Uomo Delinquente*. Torino: Bocca, 1896-97.

Lorenz, Konrad. *On Agression*. New York: Harcourt, Brace and World, Inc., 1963.

Manpower Administration, U. S. Department of Labor. *Introducing Jobs '70*. Pamphlet. Washington, D. C.: U. S. Government Printing Office, 1970.

Martindale, Don. *The Nature and Types of Sociological Theory*. Boston: Houghton Mifflin Company, 1960.

Mattos, Robert L.; Mattson, Robert H.; Walker, Hill M.; and Buckley, Nancy K. "Reinforcement and Aversive Control in the Modification of Behavior." *Academic Therapy*, V (Fall, 1969), pp. 37-51.

Mead, George H. *On Social Psychology*. Edited by Anselm Strauss. Chicago: University of Chicago Press, 1964.

Menninger, Karl. *The Crime of Punishment*. New York: The Viking Press, 1966.

Merton, Robert K. "Social Structure and Anomie." *Social Theory and Social Structure*. New York: The Free Press, 1968.

Michigan Crime and Delinquency Council. *The Saginaw Probation Demonstration Project*. Lansing, 1963.

Miller, Walter B. "The Impact of a 'Total Community' Delinquency Control Project." *Social Problems*, X (Fall, 1962), pp. 176-186.

Miller, Walter B. "Inter-Institutional Conflict As a Major Impediment to Delinquency Prevention." *Juvenile Delinquency: A Book of Readings*. Edited by Rose Giallombardo. New York: John Wiley and Sons, Inc., 1966.

Miller, Walter B. "Lower-Class Culture as a Generating Milieu of Gang Delinquency." *Journal of Social Issues*, XIV, No. 3 (1958), pp. 5-19.

"More Aid for Cities in War Against Crime." *U. S. News and World Report*, February 23, 1970, pp. 36-38.

"MES: A New Vote of Confidence." *American Teacher*, LV (September, 1970), p. 14.

Morison, Samuel E. and Commager, Henry S. Vol. I of *The Growth of the American Republic*. 5th ed. New York: Oxford University Press, 1962.

Muus, Rolf. *Theories of Adolescence*. 2nd ed. New York: Random House, 1968.

Myrdal, Gunnar. *An American Dilemma*. 2 vols. New York: McGraw-Hill Book Company, 1962.

Neary, John. "A Scientist's Variations on a Disturbing Racial Theme." *Life*, June 12, 1970, pp. 58-65.

Newman, Charles L. *Sourcebook on Probation, Parole and Pardons*. Springfield: Charles C. Thomas, 1968.

Nicholson, Clara K. *Anthropology and Education*. Foundations of Education Series. Columbus: Charles E. Merrill Publishing Company, 1968.

Ohlsen, Merle M. *Group Counseling*. New York: Holt, Rinehart and Winston, 1970.

"Opening Doors to Opportunity." *Nation's Business*, April, 1970, pp. 48-54.

Packard, Vance. *The Hidden Persuaders*. New York: Pocket Books, 1958.

"Parole Board." *Life*, July 10, 1970, pp. 54-64.

Peterson, Russel K. and Rash, Bryson B. "Industry Learns to Train the Hardcore." *Education Digest*, XXXV (October, 1969), pp. 35-37.

Pinckney, Edward R. and Pinckney, Cathy. *The Fallacy of Freud and Psychoanalysis*. Englewood Cliffs: Prentice-Hall, Inc., 1965.

Podolsky, Edward. "The Chemical Brew of Criminal Behavior." *Journal of Criminal Law and Police Science*, VL (March/April, 1955), pp. 675-678.

President's Commission on Law Enforcement and Administration of Justice. *Task Force Report: Corrections*. Washington, D. C.: U. S. Government Printing Office, 1967.

Project First Change. Columbia, 1969. South Carolina Department of Corrections.

Pulliam, John D. *History of Education in America*. Foundations of Education Series. Columbus: Charles E. Merrill Publishing Co., 1968.

Randolph, A. Philip. Foreword. *Negroes and Jobs*. Edited by Louis A. Ferman, Joyce L. Kornbluh, and J. A. Miller. Ann Arbor: The University of Michigan Press, 1968.

Riesman, David. *The Lonely Crowd*. New Haven: Yale University Press, 1961.

Riessman, Frank. *The Culturally Deprived Child*. New York: Harper and Row, 1962.

Roebuck, Julian B. *Criminal Typology*. Springfield: Charles C. Thomas Co., 1967.

Roethlisberger, F. J. and Dickson, W. J. *Management and the Worker*. Cambridge: Harvard University Press, 1939.

Rosen, Hjalmar. *A Group Orientation Approach for Facilitating the Work Adjustment of the Hard-Core Unemployed*. Unpublished Research Project sponsored by the U. S. Department of Labor, April 15, 1969.

Rosen, Hjalmar. *On-the-Job Orientation of Unemployed Skill Center Trainees and Their Supervisors*. Unpublished research project sponsored by the U. S. Department of Labor, June 1, 1970.

Rosenfield, Albert. "The Psycho-biology of Violence." *Life*, June 21, 1968, pp. 67-71.

Roucek, Joseph S. *Dictionary of Sociology*. Edited by Henry Pratt Fairchild. Totowa: Littlefield, Adams & Co., 1968.

Rutledge, Aaron L. and Gass, Gertrude Zeman. *Nineteen Negro Men*. San Francisco: Jossey-Bass, Inc., 1967.

Ruttenberg, Stanley H. "Manpower Training—The Seeds of a Dilemma." *Manpower*, I (January, 1969), pp. 3-5.

Salter, Andrew. *The Case Against Psychoanalysis.* New York: Henry Holt and Company, 1952.

Sapir, Edward. "The Status of Linguistics as a Science." *Language,* V (1929), pp. 207-214.

Schachtel, Ernest G. *Metamorphosis.* New York: Basic Books, 1959.

Schuessler, Karl F. "Parole Predictions: Its History and Status." *Journal of Criminal Law, Criminology and Police Science,* VL (December, 1954), pp. 425-431.

Schur, Edwin. *Crimes Without Victims.* Englewood Cliffs: Prentice-Hall Inc., 1965.

Sexton, Patricia C. *Education and Income.* New York: The Viking Press, 1960.

Sheldon, William H. *Varieties of Delinquent Youth: An Introduction to Constitutional Psychiatry.* New York: Harper and Brothers, 1949.

Sherif, Muzafer. *In Common Predicament.* New York: Houghton Mifflin Company, 1966.

Shibutani, Tamotsu. *Society and Personality.* Englewood Cliffs: Prentice-Hall, Inc., 1961.

Silverman, Daniel. "Clinical and Electroencephalographical Studies on Criminal Psychopaths." *Archives of Neurology and Psychiatry,* I (July, 1943), pp. 18-20, 30-31.

Smith, Henry P. *Psychology in Teaching.* Englewood Cliffs: Prentice-Hall, Inc., 1954.

Somers, Gerald G. "Training the Unemployed." *In Aid of the Unemployed.* Edited by Joseph M. Becker. Baltimore: The John Hopkins Press, 1965.

Sorokin, Pitirim. *Fads and Foibles in Modern Sociology.* Chicago: Henry Regnery Company, 1956.

Stagner, Ross and Solley, Charles M. *Basic Psychology: A Perceptual-Homeostatic Approach.* New York: McGraw-Hill Book Company, 1970.

Stagner, Ross. *Psychology of Personality.* 3rd ed. New York: McGraw-Hill Book Company, Inc., 1961.

Stuart, Richard B. *Trick or Treatment: How and When Psychotherapy Fails.* Champaign: Research Press, 1970.

Sutherland, Edwin H. and Cressey, Donald R. *Principles of Criminology.* 7th ed. New York: J. B. Lippincott Company, 1966.

Szasz, Thomas S. *Ideology and Insanity.* New York: Doubleday & Company, Inc., 1970.

Tappan, Paul W. *Crime, Justice, and Correction.* New York: McGraw-Hill Book Company, Inc., 1960.

Tappan, Paul W. "Who is the Criminal?" *American Sociological Review,* XII (February, 1947), pp. 96-102.

Terman, Sibyl and Walcutt, Charles C. *Reading: Chaos and Cure.* New York: McGraw-Hill Book Company, Inc., 1958.

Thomas, R. Murray. *Aiding the Maladjusted Pupil.* New York: David McKay Company, Inc., 1967.

Thompson, George N. *The Psychopathic Delinquent and Criminal.* Springfield: Charles C. Thomas, 1953.

Timasheff, Nicholas T. *Sociological Theory: Its Nature and Growth.* 3rd ed. New York: Random House, 1967.

"Training the 'Hard-Core'—A Top Banker Tells His Story." *U. S.*

News and World Report, August 12, 1968, pp. 51-53.
U. S. Department of Health, Education and Welfare. *Education of the Disadvantaged: An Evaluative Report on Title I Elementary and Secondary Education Act of 1965.* Washington, D. C.: U. S. Government Printing Office, 1970.
U. S. Department of Health, Education and Welfare. *Summaries of Selected Compensatory Education Projects.* Washington, D. C.: U. S. Government Printing Office, 1970.
U. S. Department of Labor. *Occupational Outlook Handbook.* Bulletin No. 1650. Washington, D. C.: U. S. Government Printing Office, 1970.
University of California School of Criminology. *The San Francisco Project: A Study of Federal Probation and Parole.* Research Report No. 14. Los Angeles: University of California, 1969.
Vold, George B. *Theoretical Criminology.* New York: Oxford University Press, 1958.
Warters, Jane. *Group Guidance.* New York: McGraw-Hill Book Company, Inc., 1960.
Washington Research Project and NAACP Legal Defense and Educational Fund, Inc. *Title I of ESEA: Is It Helping Poor Children.* 2nd ed. Washington, 1969.
Wells, Harry K. *The Failure of Psychoanalysis.* New York: International Publishers, 1963.
White, Robert W. *The Abnormal Personality.* 3rd ed. New York: The Ronald Press, 1964.
Whyte, William H., Jr. *The Organization Man.* New York: Simon and Schuster, Inc., 1956.
"Who Are the Unemployed: Grass Roots Survey?" *U. S. News and World Report,* November 16, 1970, pp. 54-57.
Williams, Edward Bennett. Statement in *U. S. News and World Report,* March 16, 1970, p. 20.
Wohl, R. Richard. "The Rags to Riches Story." *Class, Status and Power.* Edited by Reinhard Bendix and Seymore M. Lipset. 2nd ed. New York: The Free Press, 1966.
Wolf, Eleanor P. and Wolf, Leo. "Sociological Perspective on the Education of Culturally Deprived Children." *The Disadvantaged Child: Issues and Innovations.* Edited by Joe L. Frost and Glenn R. Hawkes. Boston: Houghton Mifflin Company, 1966.
Wolfe, Tom. *Radical Chic & Mau-Mauing the Flak Catchers.* New York: Farrar, Straus and Giroux, 1970.
Young Kimball. *Sociology: A Study of Society and Culture.* 2nd ed. New York: American Book Company, 1949.

SUBJECT INDEX

A

Abraham, Karl, 96
Abraham, Willard, 51
Alger, Horatio, 34
Alpern, Dr. Gerald, 80
Augmented Reading Project, 78
Augustus, John, 88

B

Ballachey, Egerton L., 17
Behavior
  ideal, 35-36, 39-41
  real, 35-36, 39-41
Behrens, Marjorie, 20
Benedict, Ruth, 18
Berman, Louis, 93
Bernstein, Basil, 59-60
Bloom, Benjamin, 57-59
Bolding, Kenneth, 169
Brody, Sylvia, 20

C

Caprio, Frank, 96
Careers in Crime Research
  Program, 113
Carver, George Washington, 121
Channen, Gloria, 81
Chase Manhattan Bank Training
  Program, 135
Childs, John, 26
Cloward, Richard A., 100
Cohen, Albert, 99-100
Compensatory education, 41,
  50-52
  analysis of, 76-82
  controversy in, 161-162
  counseling in, 149

history and scope of, 52-54
psychotherapy in, 149
Conant, James, 76
Conrad, John, 113
Cooley, Charles H., 11-12
Counseling
  analysis of, 151-159
  controversy in, 164
  definition of, 143-144
  in compensatory education,
    149
  in criminal rehabilitation, 150
  in training the hard-core
    unemployed, 150-151
  scope of, 146-147
Cressey, Donald R., 98-99
Criminal behavior, theories of
  legalistic, 90-91
  physical-constitutional-
    hereditary, 91-94
  psychological, 94-97
  sociological, 98-101
Criminal rehabilitation, 41
  analysis of, 109-114
  controversy in, 162-163
  counseling in, 150
  history and scope of, 87-90
  nature of the problem, 85-87
  process and theories of
    choice of milieu, 101-102
    diagnosis, 102-103
    treatment, 103-105
  psychotherapy in, 150
  resocialization in, 85-117
Criminal typology, 106-109
Criminolegal systems
  history of, 31-33
  institutional norms in, 31-33

socialization in, 27
Cronbach, Lee J., 158
Crutchfield, Richard S., 17
Culturally disadvantaged under-
    achiever, 50-52
    American Indian, 60-61
    causes, 54-68
    middle-class, 61-62
    rural migrant, 61
    Spanish speaking, 60

D

Denker, P. G., 156
Dewey, John, 71
Differential association, 98-99
Disadvantaged
    see culturally disadvantaged
    underachiever
Dizard, Jan E., 139
Dollard, John, 95-96
DuBois, W. E. B., 52, 121
Durkheim, Emile, 25-26

E

Economic Opportunity Act of
    1964, 53
Education
    history of, 29-31
    institutional norms in, 29-31
    resocialization in, 50-84
    socialization in, 26-27
Elementary and Secondary
    Education Act of 1965, 53
Enculturation, 25
Equitable Life Assurance Society
    of the U. S.
    training programs, 139
Eysenck, H. J., 156, 157,
    171-172

F

Fantini, Mario D., 51, 59, 61, 80
Fox, David, 81
Freeman, Roger, 80, 81-82
Freud, Sigmund, 146, 153, 154,
    155, 156

G

Gass, Gertrude Zeman, 137-138
Gazda, G. M., 152-153
Generalized other, 12-13
Gibbons, Don, 106-109
Glasser, William, 73-75
Glueck, Eleanor, 93
Glueck, Sheldon, 93
Goffman, Erving, 67-68
Gorden, Edmund, 80
Goring, Dr. Charles, 92
Greenwald, Harold, 96

H

Hall, Edward, 6
Hard-core unemployed, 118-120
    analysis of training for,
        133-141
    controversy in, 163-164
    counseling in, 150
    history and scope of training
        for, 120-122
    psychotherapy in, 150
    theories on etiology and
        treatment of, 122-133
Harrison, Gus, 112
Havighurst, Robert, 51-52
Hawthorne studies, 166
Healy, William, 94
Hello-goodbye effect, 106
Herbart, Johann, 71
Herskovits, Melville, 25
Higher Horizons Program, 53, 77
Hollingshead, August B., 158
Holt, John, 72-73

I

Iatrogenic illness, 157
Industry
    institutional norms in, 33-35
    resocialization in, 118-141
Infant Education Research
    Project, 78
Inkeles, Alex, 18-19
Institutional norms
    in criminolegal systems, 31-33
    in education, 29-31
    in industry, 33-35

J

Jensen, Arthur, 55, 168
Job Opportunities in the Business
    Sector, 121-122, 134, 138
Job Therapy, Inc., 111

K

Kardiner, Abraham, 18, 20
Kerber, August, 14-15
Kohl, Herbert, 58-59
Krech, David, 17
Kretschmer, Ernest, 93

L

Language
    acquisition of, 7-8
    defined, 10
    modes
        elaborated, 59-60
        restricted, 59-60
    nonverbal communication, 5-6
    verbal communication, 6
Larsen, Mary J., 152-153
Learning
    classical, 7-8
    conditioned response, 7-8
    conditioned stimulus, 7-8
    instrumental, 7, 8-9
    unconditioned response, 7-8
    unconditioned stimulus, 7-8
Learning disability
    causes, 54-68
    institutional, 68-78
    who, 50-52
Learning theory, 170-176
Levinson, Daniel, 18-19
Lewin, Kurt, 169-170
Liebow, Elliot, 124, 130
Lombroso, Cesare, 91-92
Looking-glass self, 11-12
Lorenz, Konrad, 6

M

McDonnell-Douglas Corporation,
    121
Malinowski, Bronislaw, 20
Mass-culture, 14-15

Mass media, effect of, 13-15
Maturation, 167
Mead, George Herbert, 5-7, 12
Mead, Margaret, 18, 20
Menninger, Karl, 27
Merton, Robert K., 14, 99
Methadone, 174-175
Midcity project, 111
More Effective Schools Program,
    81-82
Moynihan, Patrick, 130

N

Narcotics addict, 103
    treatment of, 103-104
National Alliance of Businessmen,
    121-122, 134
NAACP Legal Defense and
    Educational Fund, Inc., 79
National character, 18-20

O

Ohlin, Lloyd E., 100
Ohlsen, Merle M., 143
Omnibus Crime Control and Safe
    Streets Act of 1968, 87
Opportunities Industrialization
    Center, Inc., 133
Other-direction, 14

P

Pareto, Vilfredo, 36
Parole
    history of, 87-90
    tickets of leave, 88-89
Pavlov, Ivan, 7-8
Piaget, Jean, 70-71
Pinckney, Cathy, 154-155
Pinckney, Edward R., 154-155
Podolsky, Edward, 93
Primary group, 11
Probation
    bail, 88
    benefit of clergy, 88
    filing of cases, 88
    history of, 87-90
    judicial reprieve, 88

recognizance, 88
Project First Change, 112
Project Headstart, 53-54, 78
Prostitution, 96-97
Psychoanalysis, 145-146
Psychology
    clinical, 147
    counseling, 147
Psychotherapy
    analysis of, 151-159
    controversy in, 164
    definition of, 144-146
    in compensatory education, 149
    in criminal rehabilitation, 150
    in training the hard-core unemployed, 150-151
    scope of, 147-148
Punishment
    defined, 9

R

Reality therapy, 74
Recidivism, 85-87
Redlich, Frederick, 158
Reference group, 17-18
Resocialization
    defined, 39-41, 169
    forms of
        compensatory education, 41, 50-84
        criminal rehabilitation, 42, 85-114
        training for the hard-core unemployed, 42, 118-141
    history of, 48-49
    interpretation, 164-168
    of the current generation, 173-176
    use of counseling and psychotherapy in, 149
    versus socialization, 43-47
Riesman, David, 14
Riessman, Frank, 51, 62-64
Role Playing Group Problem Solving, 136

Rosen, Hjalmar, 135-137
Rutledge, Aaron L., 137-138

S

Saginaw Probation Demonstration Project of 1963, 110
Salter, Andrew, 153-154
San Francisco Project, 110
Sapir, Edward, 11
Schuessler, Karl, 109
Sexton, Patricia, 75-76
Sheldon, William, 92-93
Shibutani, Tamotsu, 6, 19-20
Silverman, Daniel, 94
Skinner, B. F., 8-9
Slow gifted child, 64
Smelser, Neil, 18
Smelser, William, 18
Smith, Wilfred, 14-15
Social consonance, 39-41
Socialization
    anticipatory, 17
    defined, 4-5
    function of, 24
    in criminolegal systems, 27
    in education, 26-27
    in industry, 27-28
    of the next generation, 176-177
    responsibility of, 28-29
    versus resocialization, 43-47
Societal dissonance, 35-36, 39-41
Somatotypes, 92-93
Somers, Gerald, 139
Sorokin, Pitirim, 5
Spontaneous remission, 170
Stigma, 67-68
Stuart, Richard B., 157
Sullivan, Dr. Leon, 133
Summer Upward Bound Project, 78-79
Sutherland, Edwin H., 98-99
Szasz, Thomas, 158-159

T

Tappan, Paul, 90
Terman, Sibyl, 68-70

Therapy
    behavior, 169-173
    client-centered, 145, 146
Thomas, R. Murray, 66
Thompson, George, 94
Thief, 103
    treatment of, 104-105
Trade Union Leadership Council,
    121

U

U. S. Office of Education, 80
Upward Bound, 53

W

Wahl, C. W., 20
Walcutt, Charles C., 68-70
Washington, Booker T., 52
Washington Research Project of
    the Southern Center for
    Studies in Public Policy, 79
Weber, Max, 33
Weinstein, Gerald, 51, 59, 61, 80
Wells, Harry, 156
Whyte, William, 34
Wolf, Eleanor P., 57, 79-80
Wolf, Leo, 57, 79-80
Wolf, Dr. Max, 80

X

XYY Chromosome, 93-94

Y

Young, Kimball, 4